Table of Contents

INTRODUCTION TO STOCK MARKET

T he stock market is where investors associate with buying and selling investments—most generally, stocks, which are shares of possession in an open organization. Before we dive more into the subject of stock market investing, we must have a decent and fundamental comprehension of "stock," i.e., we have to understandwhat a stock is, its advantages, and how it functions. In this way, let's start by characterizing stock.

What Is a Stock?

At the point when an individual possesses stock in an organization, the individual is known as an investor and is qualified to guarantee some portion of the organization's lingering resources and earnings (should the organization ever need to disintegrate). An investor may likewise be alluded to as a stockholder. The expressions "stock,""shares," and "value" are utilized conversely in present-day money related language. The stock market comprises of exchanges where investors can buy and sell singular shares of an organization.

Most accounts professional ways will be legitimately associated with stocks somehow, either as an advisor, a backer, or a buyer.

Advantages of Owning Stocks

There are numerous potential advantages to owning stocks or shares in an organization, including the accompanying:

1. Claim on Resources

An investor has a case on the resources of an organization it has stock in. Notwithstanding, the instances on resources are applicable just when the organization faces liquidation. On that occasion, the entirety of the organization's advantages and liabilities are checked, and after all loan bosses are paid, the investors can guarantee what is left. This is the explanation that value (stocks) investments are viewed as higher risk than an obligation (credit, advances, and bonds)–because loan bosses are paid before value holders, and if there are no advantages left after an obligation is paid, the value holders may get nothing.

2. Dividends and Capital Gains

A stockholder may likewise get earnings, which are delivered as dividends. The organization can choose the measure of dividends to be paid in one period (for example, one quarter or one year), or it can choose to hold the entirety of the earnings to grow the business further. Besides dividends, the stockholder can likewise appreciate capital increases from stock cost appreciation.

3. Power to Cast a Ballot

Another incredible element of stock possession is that investors are qualified to vote in favor of the executive's changes if the organization is fumbled. The official leading body of an organization will hold yearly gatherings to report to general organization execution. They unveiled plans for future period tasks and the executive's choices. Should investors and stockholders can't help contradicting the organization's current activity or tentative arrangements, they can arrange changes in the board or business procedure.

4. Limited Liability

Finally, when an individual claims shares of an organization, the nature of possession is constrained. Should the organization fail, investors are not by and by at risk for any misfortune.

Various Types of Stocks

Essentially, there are two kinds of stock issues: common stock shares and preferred stock shares.

Common Stock Shares

Common stock shares are, well, the most widely recognized when alluding to buying and selling stocks. The responsibility for share speaks to a case on the profits of the organization and offers the proprietor casting ballot rights to help toward the organization's administration. The basic stock is made to offer increases through capital growth.

Preferred Stocks Shares

Preferred stock capacities, much like corporate security and by and large, don't offer any democratic rights. Be that as it may, preferred stock ordinarily offers stable dividends, not at all like regular stock where the profit can be variable, pulled back, or not in any case advertised. Another insurance that is offered to preferred stock proprietors is they are paid before regular stockholders on account of the organization's liquidation.

Custom Stock Classes

Preferred and common stock are the two significant styles of stock. It is likewise feasible for companies to redo various classes of stock to fit the necessities of their investors. One reason for making share classes is so the organization can continue casting a ballot power-focused inside a specific gathering of proprietors. These various classes are frequently assigned in their trading images by including the letter A or B toward the finish of the image.

Warrant Stocks

Also, a few stocks are sold and put under warrant. A warrant regularly is set on the insiders or starting investors that claim over 10% of the organization's shares. The warrant normally expresses that the shares can't be sold for 3 to 5 years. Different sorts of warrants permit the insiders to buy increasingly stock after a given time.

To summarize everything, most stocks are given as normal. Normal stock can get variable dividends and have cast ballot rights. Preferred stock ordinarily costs more to buy yet has a profit fixed in unendingness with higher bank rights than the basic offer proprietor. Both face the risk of organizational disappointment.

What Determines Stock Price

When the first stock´s sale is finished, its cost can move autonomously of the real organization's prosperity; a current model is the out of this world stock cost for Tesla (ticker: TSLA), an organization that might be a long time from profitability.

Things being what they are, what does it cause stock costs to go up or down? The basic answer is the organic market. Value changes reflect market interest, so when a stock is considered alluring because of late accomplishment of the organization, a solid industry division, or out and out faddishness and fame—at that point, its cost goes up. On the off chance that investors are reluctant to buy a stock because of the organization wavering, a feeble industry area, or the cost being essentially excessively high, that absence of interest will make value drop. Sooner or later, the cost will move low enough that investors are again ready to buy, and the cycle will start from the very beginning once more. Value investors, similar to Warren Buffett, represent considerable authority in finding disagreeable stocks in overlooked enterprises that, despite everything, have solid earnings and a strong future, buying them (or buying the whole organization, as Buffett frequently does) and trusting that the cost will rise.

What Are the Benefits of Trading onthe Stock Market?

Investment Gains

The clearest advantage of buying or selling stocks is investment gains. It is the possibility to develop riches through value valuation for resources (stocks) that at first attracts most to invest inthe stock market with an end goal to make sure about their monetary future.

Gaining Dividends

A few stocks additionally offer the chance to procure dividends. Dividends can be an extraordinary method to acquire transient investment income, and who doesn't need another income stream?

Expansion

We should not disregard expansion, which is another significant advantage of investing in the stock market that is ignored by many. An appropriately differentiated investment portfolio permits losses in a single division of the market to be balanced by gains in another, which means the portfolio can be profitable, generally speaking.

Possession

Buying shares of stock gives investors possession in the organization. Investors get yearly reports so they can study the organization, and they can decide on corporate board individuals and different business choices. Some investor gatherings are bunches of fun, similar to Berkshire Hathaway's in Omaha, where Warren Buffet shares exceptional ideas on items from the companies he claims.

Risks of Owning Stocks

Alongside the advantages of stock proprietorship, there are likewise risks that investors need to consider, including:

1. Loss of Capital

There is no assurance that a stock's cost will climb. An investor may buy shares at $50 during an IPO yet find that the shares descend to $20 as the organization performs gravely, for instance.

2. No Liquidation Inclination

At the point when an organization exchanges, loan bosses are paid before value holders are. By and large, an organization will possibly exchange when it has almost no benefits left to work. Much of the time, it implies there will be no benefits left for value holders once loan bosses are paid off.

3. Irrelevant Capacity to Cast a Ballot

While retail investors technically have to cast ballot rights in official executive gatherings, by and by, they typically have exceptionally constrained impact or force. The larger part investor regularly decides the result of all votes at investor gatherings.

Current Stock Trading

Previously, shares were spoken to on a bit of paper as an authentication. At the point when an individual needed to buy shares, they expected to truly visit the workplace of a broker and make the exchange there, where they would get the genuine offer testaments. Today, physical offer authentications are seldom observed. Brokers keep records electronically, and an investor needs just navigate internet trading stages to buy shares.

What Influences Share Costs

Numerous components influence share costs: the worldwide economy, area execution, government approaches, cataclysmic events, and different elements. Investor notion—how investors feel about the organization's future possibilities—frequently has an enormous influence in directing cost. If investors are sure about an organization's capacity to quickly develop and, in the long run, produce huge rates of return, at that point, the organization's stock cost might be well over its current characteristic, or real, value.

Two of the most analyzed money related proportions used to assess stocks are accompanying:

Revenue Growth

Revenue growth enlightens investigators concerning the business execution of the organization's items or administrations, and for the most part, shows whether its clients love what it does.

Earnings Growth

Earnings uncover how effectively the organization deals with its activities and assets to create profits.

Revenue and earnings growth are both significant level indicators that can be utilized as references on whether to buy shares. In any case, stock examiners likewise utilize numerous other monetary proportions and instruments to assist investors with profiting from value trading.

Regardless of your activity in the money related industry, you will be associated with stocks somehow.

STOCK MARKET INVESTING

T he stock market is the place investors associate with buy and sell investments—most usually, stocks, which are shares of proprietorship in an open organization.

The stock market alludes to open markets that exist for giving, buying, and selling stocks that exchange on a stock exchange or over-the-counter. Stocks, otherwise called values, speak to fragmentary proprietorship in an organization, and the stock market is where investors can buy and sell responsibility for investible resources. A proficiently working stock market is viewed as basic to monetary advancement, as it enables companies to get to capital from the general populationrapidly.

The stock market is where shares of pubic recorded companies are exchanged. The essential market is the place companies glide shares to the overall population in the first stock´s sale (IPO) to raise capital.

If you claim a stock, you possess a bit of that organization. For instance, if you possess a portion of Starbucks stocks, congrats, you are a section proprietor of Starbucks. However, how would you buy that stock in any case? You need to go to the stock market to do that.

A stock market is where individuals buy and sell stocks. Those occur on any of numerous destinations, both physical and virtual, that are known as exchanges.

At the point when individuals make statements like, "the stock market was up/down today," they are alluding to the "stock market" as a solitary element.

They are discussing how the entirety of the stocks is doing.

History of Trade on the Stock Market

Before we plunge into how the stock market functions, we should discuss how and why the stock market appeared in any case.

The Merchants of Venice were credited with trading government protections as ahead of schedule as the thirteenth century, yet the primary real stock trading markets didn't show up until the 1500s.

As was normally the situation, the need was the mother of innovation in the arrangement of the stock market. The East India Company, which qualifies as being the primary traded on an open market organization, taking into account investors to invest in different boats. In this way, rather than financing one boat and risking all-out misfortune because of privateers, infection, and storms, they permitted investors to buy shares in various ships, so if one was lost, everything was not lost. Their prosperity prompted comparable charters being allowed to different organizations in England, France, Belgium, and the Netherlands. Bistros were their trading floor, where stocks were manually written on pieces of paper and exchanged.

Antwerp was the business focal point of Belgium, and it was commonly acknowledged that it had the world's first stock market framework. Inevitably, the first U.S. stock exchange was opened in 1791 in Philadelphia.

Reasons for the Stock Market–Capital and Investment Income

The stock market fills two significant needs. First, it gives money to companies so they can invest it to fund and grow their organizations. Suppose an organization issues one million shares of stock that at thefirst sell for $10 an offer, at that point that furnishes the organization with $10 million of capital that it can use to develop its business (less whatever expenses the organization pays for an investment bank to deal with the stock contribution). By offering stock shares as opposed to getting the capital required for an extension, the organization abstains from bringing about obligation and paying interest charges on that obligation.

The optional reason the stock market serves is to give investors—the individuals who buy stocks—the chance to partake in the profits of traded on an open market company. Investors can profit from stock purchasing in one of two different ways. A few stocks deliver standard dividends (a given measure of money per portion of stock somebody possesses). The other means investors can profit from buying stocks is through selling their stock for a profit if the stock cost increments from their price tag. For instance, if an investor buys shares of an organization's stock at $10 an offer and the cost of the stock accordingly ascends to $15 an offer, the investor would then be able to understand a half profit on their investment by selling their shares.

The Stock Market Players—Investment Banks, Stockbrokers, and Investors

There are various customary members in stock market trading:

Investment Banks

They handle the first stock's sale (IPO). What happens when an organization initially chooses to turn into a trade on an open market organization by offering stock shares.

Here's a case of how an IPO functions. An organization that desires to open up to the world offers shares to an investment bank to go about as the "financier" of the organization's underlying stock contribution. The investment bank, in the wake of looking into the organization's all-out value and thinking about what level of possession the organization wishes to give up as stock shares, handles the underlying giving of shares in the market as an end-result of a charge while ensuring the organization a decided least cost for each offer. Hence, it is to the greatest advantage of the investment bank to see that all the shares offered are sold and at the most elevated conceivable cost.

Shares offered in IPOs are usually bought by enormous institutional investors, such as annuity funds or mutual fund companies. The IPO market is known as the essential, or starting, market. When a stock has been given in the essential market, all trading in the stock from that point happens through the stock exchanges in what is known as the optional market. The expression "optional market" is somewhat deceptive since this is where the mind greater part of stock trading happens day to day.

Stockbrokers

Stockbrokers, who could conceivably additionally be going about as money related advisors, buy and sell stocks for their customers, who might be either institutional investors or individual retail investors.

Value look into examiners might be utilized by stock brokerage firms, mutual fund companies, flexible investments, or investment banks. These are people who explore traded on an open market company and endeavor to conjecture whether an organization's stock is probably going to rise or fall in cost.

Fund Supervisors or Portfolio Chiefs

Fund supervisors or portfolio chiefs, which incorporates support stock investment administrators, mutual fund directors, and exchange-exchanged fund (ETF) supervisors, are significant stock market members since they buy and sell enormous amounts of stocks. If a mainstream mutual fund chooses to invest intensely in a specific stock, that interest for the stock alone is regularly huge enough to drive the stock's cost discernibly higher.

Stock Market Indexes

The general execution of the stock market is typically followed and reflected in the presentation of different stock market indexes. Stock indexes are made out of a choice of stocks that are intended to reflect how stocks are performing by and large. Stock market indexes themselves have exchanged the type of options and prospects contracts, which are additionally exchanged on controlled exchanges.

Bull and Bear Markets, and Short Selling

Two of the essential ideas of stock market trading are "bull" and "bear" markets. The term bull market is utilized to allude to a stock market in which the cost of stocks is commonly rising. This is the kind of market most investors flourish in, as most of the stock investors are buyers, instead of short-sellers, of stocks. A bear market exists when stock costs are by and large declining in cost.

Investors can, in any case, profit even in bear markets through short selling. Short selling is the act of acquiring stock that the investor doesn't hold from a brokerage firm that owns shares of the stock. The investor, at that point, sells the obtained stock shares in the auxiliary market and gets the money from the offer of that stock. If the stock value decays as the investor trusts, at that point, the investor can obtain a profit by buying an adequate number of shares to bring back to the broker the number of shares they acquired at an all-out cost not as much as what they got for selling shares of the stock prior at a more significant expense.

For instance, if an investor accepts that the stock of organization "An"will probably decay from its current cost of $20 an offer, the investor can put down what is known as an edge store to acquire 100 shares of the stock from his broker. He, at that point, sells those shares for $20 each, the current value, which gives him $2,000. If the stock, at that point, tumbles to $10 an offer, the investor would then be able to buy 100 shares to come back to his broker for just $1,000, leaving him with a $1,000 profit.

Examining Stocks—Market Cap, EPS, and Financial Ratios

Stock market examiners and investors may take a gander at an assortment of elements to show a stock's plausible future course, up or down in cost. Here's a summary of probably the most ordinarily saw factors for stock examination.

A stock's market capitalization or market top is the all-out value of all the remarkable shares of the stock. Higher market capitalization, as a rule, shows an organization that is all the more entrenched and monetarily solid.

Traded on an open market company are required by exchange administrative bodies to give earnings reports routinely. These quarter and annual reports are deliberately watched by market examiners as a decent pointer of how an organization's business is doing so far. Among the key variables broke down from earnings reports are the organization's earnings per share (EPS), which mirrors the organization's profits as partitioned among the entirety of its exceptional shares of stock.

Experts and investors likewise habitually look at various budgetary proportions that are expected to demonstrate the monetary dependability, profitability, and growth capability of a traded on an open market organization. Coming up next are a couple of the key money related proportions that investors and experts consider:

Cost to Earnings (P/E) Ratio: The proportion of an organization's stock cost comparable to its EPS. A higher P/E proportion shows that investors are happy to follow through on greater expenses per share for the organization's stock since they anticipate that the organization should develop and the stock cost to rise.

Obligation to Equity Ratio: This is a fundamental measurement of an organization's budgetary strength, as it shows what level of an organization's tasks is being funded by obligation contrasted with what rate is being funded by value investors. A lower obligation to value proportion, demonstrating essential funding from investors, is ideal.

Profit for Equity (ROE) Ratio: The arrival on value (ROE) proportion is viewed as a decent marker of an organization's growth potential, as it demonstrates the organization's overall gain comparative with the all-out value investment in the organization.

Profit Margin: There are a few profit edges proportions that investors may consider, including working profit edge and net profit edge. The upside of taking a gander at a profit edge rather than only a flat-out dollar profit figure is that it shows what an organization's rate profitability is. For instance, an organization may show a profit of $2 million.However, if that just means a 3% profit edge, at that point, any huge decrease in revenues may compromise the organization's profitability.

Other ordinarily utilized money related proportions remember to return for resources (ROA), profit yield, the cost to book (P/B) proportion, current proportion, and the stock turnover proportion.

The Two Basic Approaches to Stock Market Investing—Value Investing and GrowthInvesting

There are innumerable techniques investigators and investors utilizefor stock picking. However, practically every one of them is some type of the two essential stock buying strategies of value investing or growth investing.

1. Value investors normally invest in settled companies that have demonstrated consistent profitability over a significant period and may offer ordinary profit income. Value investing is more centered around staying away from risk than growth investing is, although value investors do look to buy stocks when they believe the stock cost to be an undervalued deal.

2. Growth investors search out companies with uncommonly high growth potential, planning to acknowledge the most extreme gratefulness in share cost. They are normally less worried about profit income, and they are all the more ready to risk investing in generally youthful companies. Innovation stocks, given their high growth potential, are regularly preferred by growth investors.

Mutual Funds and How They Work

A mutual fund is an assortment of stocks, securities, or different protections. At the point when you buy a mutual fund, you possess the portion of the mutual fund. The cost of each mutual fund share is called its NAV or net resource value. That is the absolute value of the considerable number of protections it possesses separated by the number of the mutual fund's shares. Mutual fund shares are exchanged persistently. However, their costs change toward the finish of every business day.

Stock Funds

Stock funds center around companies that are traded on an open market on one of the stock market exchanges. Some mutual funds invest, as indicated by the organization's size. These are little, mid, or huge top funds.

Others invest in the sort of organization. Growth funds center around creative firms that are quickly extending. Value funds center around companies that others may have disregarded. Additionally, innovative funds may likewise have a lot of growth companies. Blue-chip funds additionally have many value companies. You may need a fund that centers around companies that issue dividends. Huge numbers of these are likewise blue chip or value companies.

Numerous funds center around geographic zones. Local funds just buy companies that are US-based. Universal funds can pick the best-performing nations anyplace on the planet. Outskirts markets target littler countries like Argentina, Morocco, and Vietnam. Developing market funds center around great companies in Russia, China, and different nations in the MSCI Emerging Markets Index.

You ought to invest in mutual funds rather than stocks on the off chance that you would prefer not to look into each organization's fiscal reports. Mutual funds additionally give moment broadening. Therefore, mutual funds are less risky than singular stocks. If one organization fails, at that point, you don't lose all your investment. Therefore, mutual funds give a considerable lot of the advantages of stock investing without a portion of the risks.

Security Funds

Security funds invest in protections that arrive at a fixed income. They got mainstream after the 2008 monetary emergency. Investors who were scorched during the 2008 stock market crash set out toward security. They were pulled in to securities notwithstanding record-low loan fees.

The most secure are money market funds. They buy declarations of the store, momentary Treasury bills, and other money market instruments. Since they are so protected, they offer the least return. You can get a somewhat better yield absent considerably more risk with long haul government obligations and metropolitan securities.

Better yields and higher risks happen with corporate security funds. The riskiest security funds hold high return securities. A few funds separate between present moment, medium-term, and long-haul securities. Transient funds are more secure yet have a lower return. Long haul bonds are riskier because you hold them longer. Be that as it may, they offer a better yield.

Many security funds claim similar securities. If one administrator begins selling that bond, the others will do likewise. Be that as it may, there wouldn't be a lot of buyers for those bonds. Low liquidity would drive costs down even lower. Bonds would be dependent upon a similar unpredictability as stocks and wares. It could trigger a sell-off that could devastate numerous funds. Instances of that situation happened during the bond "streak crash" in October 2014.

Effectively Managed vs. Exchange Traded Funds

Every single mutual fund is either effectively overseen or exchange-exchanged. Effectively oversaw funds have an administrator who chooses which security to buy and sell. They have an objective that controls the supervisor's investment choice. The administrator looks to outflank their record by trading protections. Subsequently, their charges are higher. These funds must surpass both the record and their higher expenses.

Exchange-exchanged funds coordinate a record. Since they needn't bother with a lot of trading, their expenses are lower. Therefore, these funds have gotten increasingly famous since the Great Recession.

Advantages and Disadvantages

Mutual funds have less risk than buying singular protections since they are a broadened investment. You aren't as reliant on an individual stock or bond, either its basic organization. If one of the companies fails, you claim a lot more stocks to ensure your investment.

Effectively oversaw funds give you the advantages of expert stock picking and the portfolio on the board. You don't need to look into a large number of companies. The directors are specialists in each field. It would be practically unthinkable for you to turn into a specialist in all the zones in which you'd prefer to invest.

Be that as it may, despite everything sets aside a lot of effort to inquire about mutual funds. To exacerbate it, the directors of funds change. At the point when that occurs, it could influence the presentation of your fund regardless of whether the division is progressing nicely. That is significant because chiefs consistently change the stocks they possess. Regardless of whether you take a gander at the outline, it probably won't reflect current stock proprietorship. You don't have the foggiest idea of what you are buying explicitly, so you depend on the mastery of the chief.

The outline cautions that past presentation is no assurance of future returns. Yet, past execution is all you need to go on. There's a decent possibility that a fund that is beaten the market in the past fails to meet expectations later on. That is particularly valid if the administrator changes. The most noteworthy hindrance is that mutual funds charge yearly administration expenses. That ensures they will cost more than the hidden stocks. These charges are frequently covered up in a few places in the plan.

To pick great mutual funds, you must comprehend your investing objectives. Are you putting something aside for retirement or saving some additional money for a stormy day? Stock funds would be best for long haul retirement investing, while a money market fund is best for momentary reserve funds.

Work with a confirmed monetary organizer. The person in question will assist you in deciding your best resource assignment and investment technique.

Mutual Fund Companies

Mutual funds are overseen by many companies, which have several funds each. Most companies center around explicit strategies to stand apart from the group. Here are the main ten biggest mutual fund companies by size, with their methodology:

1. Vanguard-Low administration expenses.

2. Fidelity-Full budgetary administrations.

3. American-Conservative investment strategies with long haul investment time allotment.

4. Barclays-Targets proficient, not singular, investors.

5. Franklin Templeton-Bonds, developing markets, and value companies.

6. PIMCO-Bond funds.

7. T. Rowe Price-No-heap funds.

8. State Street-Targets proficient, not singular, investors.

9. Oppenheimer-Actively oversaw funds.

10. Dodge and Cox-Long-term investment time.

How the Stock Market Functions

The idea of driving how the stock market functions are entirely basic. Working a lot of like a bartering house, the stock market empowers buyers and sellers to arrange costs and make exchanges.

The stock market works through a system of exchanges. Companies list shares of their stock on an exchange through a procedure called the first sale of stock, or IPO. Investors buy those shares, which permits the organization to fund-raise to develop its business. Investors would then be able to buy and sell these stocks among themselves, and the exchange tracks the organic market of each recorded stock.

That organic market help decide the cost for every security or the levels at which stock market members—investors and traders—are happy to buy or sell. PC calculations, by and large, do the majority of those computations.

Buyers offer an "offer," or the most noteworthy amount they're willing to pay, which is typically lower than the amount sellers "ask" for in exchange. This distinction is known as the offer-ask spread. For an exchange to happen, a buyer needs to build his cost, or a seller needs to diminish hers.

Verifiably, stock exchanges likely occurred in a physical marketplace. Nowadays, the stock market works electronically through online stockbrokers. Each exchange occurs on a stock-by-stock premise, yet generally speaking, stock costs regularly move the couple on account of news, political occasions, financial reports, and different components.

Those hoping to buy put in a request through a mediator known as a "broker," expressing what they are set up to pay per offer and what number of shares they wish to buy. That request is known, in-market language, as an "offer." Thus, those expecting to sell their stock submit a request expressing what number of shares they are hoping to sell and at what value, known as "offer" or "ask" cost.

At the point when buyers and sellers concede to a value, the exchange matches them, and that is posted as the cost of the stock. The costs you see, along these lines, are just the last cost at which a deal happened. The stock market works like a closeout where investors buy and sell shares of stocks. These are a little bit of responsibility for the open organization. Stock costs, as a rule, mirror investors' assessment of what the organization's earnings will be.

Traders who figure the organization will do all around offer the cost up, while the individuals who trust it will do inadequately offer the cost down. Sellers attempt to get much as could reasonably be expected for each offer, ideally making substantially more than what they paid for it.However, buyers attempt to get the least cost so that they can sell it for a profit later.

The Most Effective Method to Invest in the Stock Market

Normal investors can't exchange on the stock market legitimately. Rather, they should employ a broker-dealer to execute the exchanges. There's a wide assortment of decisions:

- Fee-just monetary counselors who charge a yearly expense, typically 1% of advantages.

- Online dealers like E-Trade, who charge a little expense for each exchange.

- Large banks, similar to Goldman Sachs or Well Fargo Advisors, give monetary arranging notwithstanding executing exchanges.

- Small brokers who simply execute orders.

Numerous investors buy stocks through mutual funds. These are companies that buy an assortment of stocks. Many investors buy shares in the mutual fund as opposed to owning the stocks themselves. They exploit the mutual fund administrator's aptitude. Since there are such huge numbers of stocks, this broadened investment has a lower risk than a solitary stock.

The vast majority of the stocks exchanged are regular stocks. Be that as it may, a few investors buy favored stocks. They deliver a settled upon profit at ordinary interims, and they don't have to cast a ballot right. They are less risky; however, they additionally offer a little return.

Where Is the Stock Market?

The two biggest exchanges on the planet are both in the United States. The New York Stock Exchange records 2,400 companies. Consolidated, they are worth around $21 trillion in market capitalization. That is the value of every one of its shares. The NYSE is situated on Wall Street. The Nasdaq stock market has 3,800 companies with a market top of $11 trillion. It's situated in Times Square.

Each exchange matches buyers with sellers. However, they do it another way. The NYSE is a genuine sales management firm. It coordinates the most elevated offer at the least deals cost. There is a market creator for each stock who will fill in the hole to ensure exchanges go easily. At the Nasdaq, buyers and sellers exchange with a dealer rather than one another. It's done electronically, so exchanges occur in split seconds.

The BATS Global Marketplace was shaped to make a progressively proficient innovation. Its objective was to stay away from a blazing crash like the one that hit the NASDAQ.

There are additionally numerous little exchanges to serve explicit sorts of traders. For instance, "Dim Pools," like Liquidnet, take into account high-volume, visit traders like flexible investments. Dim Pools conceal their customer's strategies from the challenge. They guarantee their secrecy as well as enormous coordinate requests to stay away from doubt.

The significant nations have their own stock exchanges for their local enterprises. The five greatest are London, Tokyo, Shanghai, Hong Kong, and Euronext exchanges.

Current Stock Market

The stock markets use files to report their current conditions. The main three are the Dow Jones Industrial Averages, the S&P 500, and the Nasdaq. The DJIA tracks the stock costs of the best 30 U.S. companies. The Nasdaq stock tracks the stocks on its exchange. Each of these likewise has numerous littler files that track explicit parts of the companies they track. For instance, the Nasdaq 100 tracks the biggest stocks on its exchange.

Each exchange, far and wide, has a record that writes about its current status. The records for the best five exchanges are the FTSE 100, Nikkei 225, Shanghai Stock Exchange, Hang Seng, and the Euronext 100.

What's more, numerous records report on different kinds of companies recorded on the exchanges. The Russell 2000 reports on 2,000 little top companies. The MSCI Index gives an account of developing market companies.

Focal Points

Companies sell stocks since it's a decent method to get a tremendous total of budgetary capital. Nonetheless, the organization itself must create a great deal of income to make it beneficial. Giving an Initial Public Offering is over the top expensive. From that point forward, there is no security, as investors survey the organization's profits and procedures each quarter. Different methods for acquiring financing are private, through close to home advances or private investors, or through bonds, which are advances exchanged freely.

The upside of stocks versus bonds is that a stock doesn't require a month-to-month reimbursement of intrigue.

People utilize the stock market because the profits, by and large, outpace those of different investments, for example, securities or items. Stock market investing is an astounding method to ensure your investments show improvement over expansion.

The Stock Market Isn't the Economy but Does Affect It

The stock market adds to the U.S. economy. On the off chance that investors accept the economy is developing, they will invest in stocks at that point. That is because a solid economy assists companies with improving their earnings. That is known as a bull market. It, for the most part, happens alongside the extension period of the business cycle. Most products likewise progress admirably. That is because extending organizations will request more oil, copper, and other characteristic merchandise.

On the off chance that investors think the economy is easing back or stale, they will invest in bonds, which are a more secure investment. That is because bonds give a fixed return over the life of the advance. Bonds do well during the constriction period of the business cycle. At the point when bonds progress nicely, stocks lose value. That is known as a bear market, and it normally keeps going ayear and a half. The last bear market was from December 2007 to March 2009.

If there are dangers to the worldwide economy, investors also push toward gold and other refuge places. That typically occurs alongside a stock market amendment, when offer costs drop 10 percent or more. It's significantly increasingly evident in a stock market crash when stocks can lose that much in a day. An awful accident could even reason a downturn.

Impacts on the Stock Market

Different elements go into the choices of traders and investors about where to buy and sell singular stocks. The most significant is the profitability of the organization, as well as its possibilities for profits later on.

In an increasingly broad sense, vacillations in "the market" are essentially the whole of every one of those individual stock choices. However, some things direct the bearing of the market as a rule. To comprehend them, you should comprehend a certain something: the market is a forward-limiting instrument.

In layman's terms, traders are continually looking for advances. They use past value activity as charts to illuminate their choices to sell or buy; however, what chooses whether they settle on the correct choice or not is the thing that will occur later on.

What's to come isn't known, yet a few things are utilized to decide the probability of a stock's cost going up or down. Huge numbers of those things, for example, financial quality and political security, influence all stocks, so changes in the monetary conditions, political dependability, and geopolitical soundness can cause far-reaching buying or selling, and along these lines wide market moves.

How Would You Buy Stocks?

You need two things to take an interest in the stock market:

1. Money
2. A broker

For the vast majority, those two things are consolidated in a retirement account. They, and frequently their manager, add to a record at a brokerage that is then invested, typically in any event incompletely in stocks, for their retirement.

If you need to take an interest all the more effectively in the market, however, your retirement account isn't the best spot to do it, nor are your retirement funds the best activity it with, because losses, some of the time considerable losses, are constantly a chance.

To begin, you will require a brokerage account. In the not-so-distant past, that implied utilizing and paying for an individual at a brokerage firm to offer you data and guidance and, all the more significantly, to put in exchange requests for your sake.

Presently, however, data is openly accessible on the web, similar to a brokerage account with moderately low exchange charges. It is anything but difficult to open one. However, that doesn't imply that it ought to be managed without thought. In addition to the fact that fees vary extensively, the accessible devices and exhortation and speed and closeness to your request for execution can likewise do as such.

Different Types of Markets

In the exchange of benefits, there are a few unique sorts of markets to encourage exchange. Each market works under various trading components, which influence liquidity and control.

These three are the primary kinds of markets:

1. Dealers (Over-the-counter)

2. Exchanges

3. Brokers

Dealer Markets

A dealer market works with a dealer that goes about as a counterparty for the two buyers and sellers. The dealer sets to offer and approaches costs for the security being referred to and will exchange with any investor ready to acknowledge those costs. Protections sold by dealers are here and there known as exchanged over-the-counter (OTC).

In doing such, the dealer gives liquidity in the market at the expense of a little premium. After the closing of a day, dealers will regularly set lower-cost offers than the market, and then they will ask for higher costs. The spread between these costs is the profit the dealer makes. Consequently, the dealer accepts the counterparty risk.

Dealer markets are less normal in stocks, however, increasingly basic insecurities and money. Dealer markets are additionally proper for prospects and options or other institutionalized agreements and subsidiaries. At long last, the outside exchange market is normally worked through dealers, with banks and cash exchanges going about as the dealer go-between.

Of the three kinds of markets, the dealer market is normally the most fluid.

Broker Markets

A brokered market works by finding a counterparty to the two buyers and sellers. At the point when dealers go about as the counterparty, the postponement with brokers finding a suitable counterparty brings about less liquidity in brokered markets.

Customarily, stock markets were brokered. Stockbrokers would attempt to locate a proper counterparty for their customers on the trading floor. This is the cliché picture that Wall Street used to be known for, with people in suits shouting at one another while holding bits of paper to note their customers' requests.

Broker markets are utilized for all way of protections, particularly those with beginning issues. An IPO, for instance, will, for the most part, be propelled through an investment bank, which brokers the issue attempting to discover supporters. This is likewise comparable to new bond issues. At long last, brokered markets are additionally proper for custom-made or custom items.

Exchanges

Of the three kinds of markets, the exchange is the most mechanized; in any case, if no buyers and sellers can meet as far as value, no exchanges execute. The stock market is never again a brokered market, having changed to being a robotized exchange. Exchanges are executed dependent on request books that coordinate buyers with sellers.

The benefit of the exchange is arranging a focal area for buyers and sellers to locate their own counterparties. Exchanges are mechanized, requiring no broker or dealer middle person. Exchanges are generally proper for institutionalized protections: these incorporate stocks, securities, fates, agreements, and options. Exchanges will commonly indicate qualities for the protections exchanged on the exchange.

Exchange Characteristics

- Contract or Lot Size
- Contract Execution/Trading Months
- Tick Size
- Delivery Terms
- Quality

Conveyance terms and quality are not normal in stock exchanges or bond exchanges. In a stock exchange, all that is expressed is the agreement and tick size, just as the execution. Execution is, for the most part, prompt. Agreement sizes may require a base. For instance, a stock may just be bought in heaps of 100 on a specific exchange. Tick size is normally the most minimal division of cash. In US stock exchanges, the most minimal tick in cost is a penny. An agreement tick size under this game plan would then be $1 ($0.01 x 100 shares for each parcel).

Conveyance terms and quality are all the more fittingly utilized in ware exchanges and with subsidiaries, including resources that have these attributes. Gold and precious stones, for instance, have characteristics and appraisals. Also, the physical resource must be in a structure deliverable to the buyer or agreement holder. These attributes are indicated by the exchange.

HOW TO START INVESTING IN THE STOCK MARKET

Investing in stocks is an amazing method to develop riches. Be that as it may, how would you begin? Follow the means beneath to figure out how to invest in the stock market.

1. Choose How You Need to Invest in Stocks

There are different ways to move toward stock investing. Pick the option beneath that best speaks to how you need to invest and how hands-on you'd prefer to be in singling out the stocks you invest in.

• "I'm the DIY type and am keen on picking stocks and stock funds for myself." Keep perusing; this article separates things hands-on investors need to know. Or on the other hand, if you definitely realize the stock-buying game and simply need a brokerage, see our gathering of the best online stock brokers.

• "I realize stocks can be an incredible investment, yet I'd like somebody to deal with the procedure for me." Essentially the entirety of the significant brokerage firms offers these administrations, which invest your money for your dependent on your particular objectives. When you incline the top of the priority list, you're prepared to search for a record.

2. Open an Investing Account

By and large, talking, to invest in stocks, you need an investment account. For the hands-on types, this generally implies a brokerage account. For individuals that need little assistance, opening a record through a Robo-advisor is a reasonable option. We separate the two procedures underneath.

Significant: A 401(k) is a sort of investment account, and in case you're taking an interest in one, you may as of now be investing in stocks, likely through mutual funds. Be that as it may, a 401(k) won't offer you access to singular stocks, and your decision in mutual funds will probably be very restricted. Manager coordinating dollars make it worth contributing notwithstanding a constrained investment choice, yet once you're sufficiently contributing to acquiring that coordinate, you can think about investing through different records.

TheDIY Option: Opening a Brokerage Account

An online brokerage account likely offers your speediest and most economical way of buying stocks, funds, and an assortment of different investments. You may open an individual retirement account with a broker, otherwise called an IRA—here are our top picks for IRA accounts—or you can open an assessable brokerage account in case you're now sparing satisfactorily for retirement somewhere else.

The Passive Option: Opening a Robo-Advisor Account

A Robo-advisor offers the advantages of stock investing yet doesn't require its proprietor to do the legwork required to pick singular investments. Robo-advisor administrations give total investment to the board: These companies will get some information about your investment objectives during the onboarding procedure and afterward assemble a portfolio intended to accomplish those points.

This may sound costly. However, the administration expenses here are commonly a small amount of the expense of what a human investment supervisor would charge. For this, most Robo-advisors charge only 0.25% to 0.50% of your benefits under administration. What's more, yes—you can likewise get an IRA at a Robo-advisor on the off chance that you wish.

3. Realize the Contrast among Stocks and Stock Mutual Funds

Going to the DIY course? Try not to stress. Stock investing doesn't need to be entangled. For a great many people, stock market investing implies picking among these two investment types:

- **Stock mutual funds or exchange-exchanged funds.** These mutual funds let you buy little bits of a wide range of stocks in a solitary exchange. Record funds and ETFs are a sort of mutual fund that tracks a file; for instance, a Standard and Poor's 500 fund duplicates that list by buying the stock of the companies in it. At the point when you invest in a fund, you likewise possess little bits of every one of those companies. You can assemble a few funds to construct an expanded portfolio. Note that stock mutual funds are likewise now and then called value mutual funds.

- **Individual stocks.** If you're after a particular organization, you can buy a solitary offer or a couple of shares as an approach to plunge your toe into the stock-trading waters. Building a broadened portfolio out of numerous individual stocks is conceivable, yet it takes a huge investment.

The advantage of stock mutual funds is that they are innately broadened, which decreases your risk. Be that as it may, they're probably not going to ascend in fleeting style as some individual stocks would. The upside of individual stocks is that an astute pick can pay off abundantly. However, the chances that any individual stock will make you rich are exceedingly thin.

By far, most investors—especially the individuals who are investing their retirement reserve funds—building a portfolio made essentially out of mutual funds is a reasonable decision.

4. Set a Budget for Your Stock Investment

New investors frequently have two inquiries right now the procedure:

1. **How a lot of cash do I have to begin investing in stocks?** The measure of money you have to buy an individual stock relies upon how costly the shares are. (Offer costs can go from only a couple of dollars to two or three thousand dollars.) If you need mutual funds and have a small budget, an exchange-exchanged fund (ETF) might be your most logical option. Mutual funds regularly have

essentials of $1,000 or more. However, ETFs exchange like a stock, which implies you buy them at an offer cost—at times, under $100).

2. **How a lot of cash would it be a good idea for me to invest in stocks?** In case you're investing through funds—have we referenced this as our inclination? —you can apportion a genuinely huge part of your portfolio toward stock funds, particularly if you make some long memories skyline. A 30-year-old investing for retirement may have 80% of their portfolio in stock funds; the rest would be in security funds. Singular stocks are another story.

5. Begin Investing

Stock investing is loaded up with many-sided strategies and approaches, yet the absolute best investors have done minimal more than stay with the nuts and bolts. That by and large methods utilizing funds for the main part of your portfolio—Warren Buffett has broadly said a minimal effort S&P 500 record fund is the best investment most Americans can make—and picking singular stocks just on the off chance that you have faith in the organization's potential for long haul growth.

If individual stocks offer to you, figuring out how to investigate stocks merits your time. On the off chance that you intend to stick essentially with funds, fabricating a basic arrangement of wide-based, minimal effort options ought to be your objective.

The Investment Portfolio: What It Is and How to Build a Good One

Like any industry, investing has its own language. What's more, one term individuals frequently use without truly clarifying it is "investment portfolio."

Think about an investment portfolio as the manager of every one of your investments. Similarly, as you would utilize a safe to store significant reports, your investment portfolio stores all the advantages you claim—stocks, securities, mutual funds, exchange-exchanged funds, etc. In contrast to a sheltered, an investment portfolio is, to a greater degree, an idea than a physical thing.

In any case, understanding what an investment portfolio is, it doesn't disclose to you much about how to assemble one. This is what you have to know.

What's Remembered for an Investment Portfolio

You may have numerous records with different budgetary investments in them yet use them for various purposes—a 401(k) for retirement versus a brokerage represents fiddling with stock trading, for instance. Be that as it may, think about your investment portfolio as an umbrella term for the entirety of your investments in the accompanying kinds of records:

- A 401(k) or another business supported arrangement.
- A singular retirement account.
- A self-coordinated, assessable brokerage account.
- An account with a Robo-advisor.
- Money market cash held in bank accounts, money market accounts, or invested in declarations of the store.
- Peer-to-peer loaning accounts.

While you may consider different things as investments (your home, autos, or craftsmanship, for instance), those aren't viewed as a major aspect of an investment portfolio. Or maybe, talking the accompanying kinds of benefits.

- Stocks.
- Bonds.
- Exchange-exchanged funds.
- Mutual funds.
- Target-date retirement funds.
- Real domain investment trusts.
- Futures.
- Options.
- Alternative investments.
- Forex.
- Short-term investments.
- Cryptocurrencies.
- Employee stock options.

The Most Effective Method to Fabricate a Wise Investment

Portfolio

Enhancement is the way to progress when investing. Spreading your money around diminishes in general risk by guaranteeing your portfolio's exhibition isn't excessively reliant on any one specific resource.

In any case, expansion doesn't mean you need to step into extraordinary resources. Rather, we prescribe utilizing minimal effort list funds (mutual funds or ETFs) for the main part of your portfolio's investments. That is because these funds track wide indexes, for example, the S&P 500, and offer a simple method to accomplish that exceedingly significant enhancement inexpensively.

Broadening also implies investing in various resources that aren't profoundly connected, which means they don't move in lockstep. Stocks and bonds have had a negative relationship since the 1990s, so when stock costs have gone up, bond costs have gone down and the other way around.

You may have heard proposals about how a lot of cash to assign to stocks versus bonds. Regularly referred to general guidelines propose subtracting your age from 100 or 110 to choose how your portfolio ought to be invested. In case you're 30, these principles recommend 70%–80% of your portfolio distributed to stocks and 20%–30% of your portfolio to bonds. In your 60s, that blend movement to 40%-half assigned to bonds and half 60% to stocks.

A few people, despite everything, like that general guideline, yet others see it as too shortsighted because it disregards your risk resistance. Whatever blend of stocks and securities you choose is directly for your portfolio, such expansion can be accomplished utilizing the ease file funds referenced previously? You don't have to swim into the universe of individual stocks or bonds on the off chance that you would prefer not to.

At last, if this feels like more than you need to choose, a portfolio the executive's administration called a Robo-advisor would settle on all these designation choices for you. After you answer a couple of inquiries concerning your investment objectives and risk resilience, these mechanized investing administrations will construct and deal with your portfolio for a moderately minimal effort.

Have a Ton of Fun with Your Portfolio

A few people are content with a set-it-and-overlook investing procedure, while others favor a hands-on approach. In any case, we prescribe organizing minimal effort record funds for the lion's share of your investment portfolio. Indeed, even proficient investors who pick stocks professionally frequently utilize these funds for their own investments.

Except if you intend to commit a great deal of time following the market, we prescribe that you keep progressively risky wagers (trading stocks, options, fates, or different resources for) close to 10% of your portfolio's value. Why? Once more, you need to secure your savings on the off chance that a "definite wager" ends up being a failure.

STEP-BY-STEP GUIDE TO START INVESTING IN THE STOCK MARKET

Stock Investment Strategies

There are various approaches to move toward stock investing, yet almost every one of them falls under one of three fundamental styles: value investing, growth investing, or file investing. These stock investment strategies follow the mentality of an investor, and the system they use to invest is influenced by various variables, for example, the investor's budgetary circumstance, investing objectives, and risk resistance.

Value Investing Basics

The procedure of value investing, in basic terms, implies buying stocks of companies that the marketplace has undervalued. The objective isn't to invest in no-name companies that haven't been perceived for their latent capacity—that falls more in the scene of theoretical or penny stock investing. Value investors commonly buy into solid companies that are trading at low costs that an investor accepts don't mirror the organization's actual value. Value investing is tied in with getting the best arrangement, like getting an incredible rebate on an architect brand.

At the point when we state that a stock is undervalued, we imply that an examination of their financial reports demonstrates that the value the stock is trading at is lower than it ought to be, founded on the organization's inherent value. This may be demonstrated by, for example, a low-cost to-book proportion (a money related proportion supported by value investors) and a high-profit yield, which speaks to the sum in dividends an organization pays out every year comparative with the cost of each offer.

The marketplace isn't constantly right in its valuations, and hence stocks regularly basically exchange for not exactly their actual worth, at any rate for a while. If you seek after a value investing system, the objective is to search out these undervalued stocks and scoop them up at a good cost.

Value Investing Long-Term

The value investing procedure is truly direct, yet rehearsing this technique is more required than you may suspect, particularly when you're utilizing it as a long-haul methodology. It's critical to stay away from the impulse to attempt to make quick money dependent on unusual market trends. A value investing methodology depends on buying into solid companies that will keep up their prosperity, and that will, in the end, have their inherent worth perceived by the markets.

Warren Buffet, one of the best and most productive value investors of the century, broadly stated, "for the time being, the market is a ubiquity challenge. In the long haul, a market is a gauging machine." Buffet bases his whole stock decisions on the genuine potential and soundness of an organization, taking a gander at the entire of each organization rather than just taking a gander at an undervalued sticker price that the market has allocated to a singular share of the organization's stock. Be that as it may, he does, in any case, want to buy stocks he sees as "on special."

The Basics of Growth Stock Investment Strategies

For a considerable length of time, growth investing has been held as the yin to value investing's yang. While growth investing is, in the essential terms, the supposed "inverse" of value investing, many value investors additionally utilize a growth investing mentality when choosing stocks. Growth investing is fundamentally the same as, in the long haul, value stock investing strategies. Essentially, in case you're investing in stocks dependent on the inborn value of an organization and its capability to develop, later on, you're utilizing a growth investing procedure.

Growth investors are recognized from carefully value investors by their emphasis on youthful companies that have demonstrated their potential for critical, better than expected growth. Growth investors take a gander at companies that have more than once demonstrated signs of growth and significant or fast increments in business and profit.

The general hypothesis behind growth investing is that the growth in earnings or revenue an organization creates will, at that point, be reflected by an expansion in share costs. Varying from value investors, growth investors may regularly buy stocks estimated at or higher than an organization's current inborn worth, because of the conviction that a proceeded with high growth rate will, in the long run, support the organization's characteristic value to a considerably more elevated level, well over the current offer cost of the stock.

Most loved money related measurements utilized by growth investors incorporate earnings per share (EPS), profit edge, and profit for value (ROE).

A Fusion of Value and Growth

In truth, in case you're thinking about a long-haul way to deal with investing, a combination of value and growth investing, as Buffet so viably utilizes, might merit your thought. There are valid justifications to back up taking these stock investment strategies.

Truly, value stocks are generally the stocks of companies in cyclical industries, which are, to a great extent, made up of organizations delivering products and enterprises that individuals utilize their optional income on. The aircraft business is a genuine model; individuals fly more when the business cycle is on an uptrend and fly less when it swings downward because they have more and less optional income, separately. Given regularity, value stocks normally perform well in the market during times of financial recuperation and thriving. However, they are probably going to fall behind when a bull market is continued for a significant time.

Growth stocks normally perform better when loan fees drop and companies' earnings take off. They are likewise commonly the stocks that keep on rising even in the late phases of a long-haul bull market. Then again, these are generally the principal stocks to get hammered when the economy eases back down.

A combination of growth and value investing offers you the chance to appreciate better yields on your investment while diminishing a generous measure of your risk. Hypothetically, on the off chance that you utilize both a value investing technique for buying a few stocks while utilizing a growth investing system for buying different stocks, you can produce ideal earnings during, for all intents and purposes, any financial cycle and any changes in returns will be bound to adjust in support of you after some time.

Passive Index Investing

List investing is a significantly more passive type of investing when contrasted with that of either value or growth investing. Subsequently, it includes far less work and strategizing concerning the investor. Record investing expands an investor's money generally among different kinds of values, planning to reflect indistinguishably comes back from the general stock market. One of the primary attractions of file investing is that numerous investigations have demonstrated that a couple of strategies of picking singular stocks beat file investing over the long haul.

A record investing technique is normally trailed by investing in mutual funds or exchange-exchanged funds that are intended to mirror the exhibition of a significant stock file, for example, the S&P 500 or the FTSE 100.

Regardless of whether you need to begin trading stocks effectively or simply need to invest as long as possible, there are things you have to know before beginning. Realizing what's in store and what apparatuses you need will help plan you so your entrance into stock trading goes as easily as could be expected under the circumstances. Here are five activities before you begin trading stocks.

Familiarize Yourself with the Stock Market

Stocks are little bits of an organization. The stock cost (additionally called a "share") mirrors the value of the organization, and its viewpoint, as dictated by the individuals trading the stock (traders and investors). Stocks don't have a set value; they constantly vary, each second of every day.

Stocks exchange on an exchange, for example, the New York Stocks Exchange (NYSE), which has long stretchedfrom 9:30 a.m. to 4:00 p.m. Eastern time. Most buying and selling of stocks happen during these hours, albeit some trading occurs outside these hours; it's called pre-market and twilight trading.

To explore the stock and inevitably make an exchange, you'll require the stock's "ticker" image. On the off chance that the organization you are investigating is traded on an open market, then you can type the organization name followed by "quote" into your preferred internet searcher, and you'll likely recover the ticker image in the outcomes. Tickers are one to five-letter codes used to exchange the stock.

You can buy stocks and afterward attempt to sell them after time has gone at a more significant expense to make a profit. It is likewise conceivable to sell first. The last process is called short selling; transient traders do it constantly, while longer-term investors will, in general, avoid it.

Before you start, familiarize yourself with the Bid/Ask Spread, as this is how costs move. Additionally, gain proficiency with the nuts and bolts of perusing a stock chart and stock statements.

Build up Your Purpose for Trading

Build up what you look for from your trading. Is it something you need to do each day? Would you like to exchange several times each week? Perhaps do some research in the evening if you have full-time work. Or, on the other hand, would you like to buy stocks and hold them as long as possible? There is no correct here. Do every one of them or one of them. Day trading is taking exchanges that last not exactly a day, and exchanges frequently just last minutes. Swing trading is taking exchanges that last from a day to a few weeks. Investing is taking exchanges that last numerous months or even years. Prior to concluding which to seek after, think about your funds.

Think about Your Finances

If you need to day trade stocks in the U.S., you have to keep up an equalization of in any event $25,000 in your account.5 If that is unrealistic, it precludes day trading.

Swing trading doesn't have a base capital necessity, yet to have the option to exchange stocks of fluctuating cost, as circumstances become accessible, you may need at any rate $10,000 focused on the undertaking. In the case of taking standard exchanges, a littler record than this is powerless to be shaved away by commissions and expenses (what the broker charges for trading, examined beneath).

Investing requires less capital. Since the exchange is held for an extensive period, commissions are not as quite a bit of a factor. Consequently, you can start to buy stocks when you can manage the cost of 100 shares (stocks normally exchange 100 squares) of the stock you are keen on. Get a good deal on commissions by making one exchange rather than different exchanges. For instance, rather than buying 100 shares each week, set aside the cash for a month and make one bigger buy.

This possibly applies if the value of the exchange is little, where the commission could speak to a noteworthy level of the capital being conveyed (over 1% is huge). Then again, on the off chance that you are buying a great many dollars' worth of stock on every investment, the commissions are, to a great extent, insignificant.

Locate a Broker and Trading Platform

A broker encourages trading between market members, permitting you to buy stocks from sellers and sell stock to buyers (buyers and sellers for each exchange). As a dealer, you need a broker that is:

- Low cost (low commissions and charges).
- Reliable (can exchange when you need, with insignificant framework blackouts).
- Honest (won't take your money or take part in risky practices with it).
- A broker who gives you apparatuses for inquiring about (least significant, since there are heaps of free instruments accessible on the web).

If you need to day exchange, there are a couple of more things you may need in a broker.

- The broker ought to execute arrangements in a split second without mediation on their part. Indeed, even a one-second deferral is excessive.

- "Trade from chart" capacities or potential capacity to quickly put in, change and drop orders.

There are heaps of brokers, some of which are better for investors and some which are better for day traders or swing traders. Picking a broker is the greatest exchange of all; all your capital is given to this organization. Invest energy inquiring about the above components before picking a broker.

Each broker offers a trading stage. This is the innovation that permits you to see stock statements, see charts, do examine, and in particular, spot orders. Test out different stages by opening demo accounts with different brokers.

Practice Before Depositing Money

As you limit your determination of brokers by messing about in their demo accounts, work on setting exchanges. Become acclimated to the different request types accessible. Start defining strategies and testing them on verifiable value charts. Spot counterfeit money exchanges dependent on those strategies and break down the discoveries with insights to check whether the methodology is probably going to deliver a profit.

There is little reason for squandering genuine money on the off chance that you can't make a profit trading counterfeit money. Then again, delivering counterfeit money returns doesn't really mean genuine money profits will come simply. There are contrasts between demo trading and genuine trading. Demo trading is as yet an entirely significant device. However, in the demo account, practice legitimate risks the executives. Risk the board is the place you just risk a limited quantity of the record on any single exchange.

THE STOCK MARKET TREND/PHASES

Including Market on the Rise Confirmed, Rise Under Pressure, and Market in Correction

Dow Industrial Average, 2001 to 2004

Investors who saw the turn in the stock market by watching the day by day decrease in the Dow Industrial and Transportation Averages and who tuned in to the market assessments given by numerous experts before June would almost certainly have made some defensive move. The market expectation had been filled by enthusiasm for tech stocks. When the tech stock air pocket went to an unexpected end, so did the market rally. The market adjustment was more serious than anticipated because of the solid selling impacts of modified trading. Some would state the market became oversold, as appeared by a snappy recuperation.

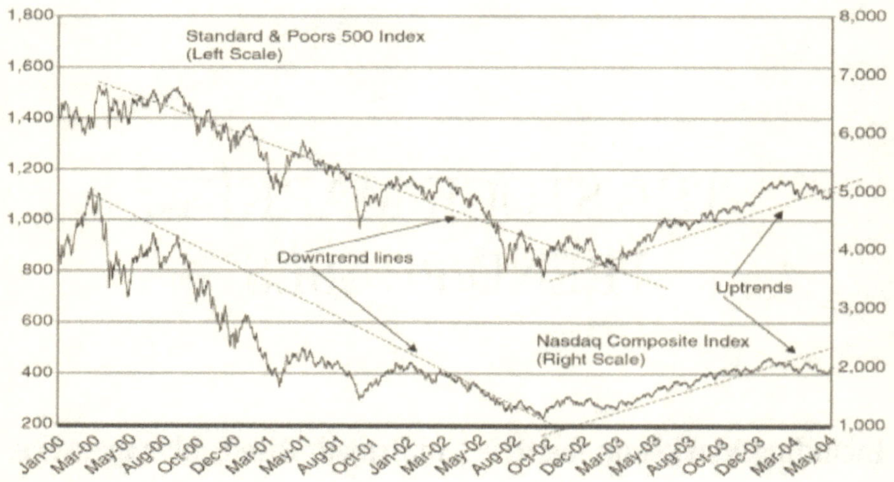

Stock Moves: Down

Buying a vehicle, a PC, or another TV, just to see it at a bargain the next week, can be a major wellspring of disturbance. Obviously, similar remains constant for stocks. To pay $52 an offer one day, at that point to hear some negative news and see a cost of $42 the following week, is definitely not a charming encounter. On the off chance that the investor's exploration and determination are substantial, the cost will likely recuperate and move to new highs. However, the value of harm in transit down can be hard to persevere. An intriguing marvel can happen with a stock value that seems to continue dropping.

As the value decays, investors will seem to buy up shares at apparent deal costs. If enough of these deal trackers show up, they can stop the value drop, yet sellers may overwhelm them. The base is the place the value quits declining and goes level or starts to remember its upward trend.

On Sale, Limited Time Only

Numerous investors consider a market "plunge,""pullback,""amendment," or "bear market" a buying opportunity. The cost is lower, and the stocks on special.

Get Information Before You Invest, Not After

The Purposes behind a value decrease can be not kidding; lower earnings or appraisals are anticipated, FICO assessments are brought down, or a potential claim or expense issue has been created. The explanation behind a value decay probably won't be so genuine: market remedy, profit-taking, worker stock dispersion, or no news related reason by any means. Whatever the purpose behind a stock value move, it very well may be beneficial to discover why it is moving before investing.

Data about a stock being referred to can be acquired from the news media, the Internet, or by calling the organization legitimately. Calling the organization may be troublesome if several different investors are attempting to do something very similar. Regularly calling the stockbroker or checking a news administration on a PC will give the appropriate response. Realizing why a stock is declining in cost can empower the investor to shape a methodology of buy, hold, or sell.

Stock Moves: Sideways

Once more, approach questions and quest for answers. For what reason isn't the stock cost moving? If other comparative stocks and the market are progressing admirably, there is a purpose behind an absence of development in a given stock. Has there been awful news as of late that has made the absence of investor premium, or is the stock currently a jewel standing by to be found?

Albeit uncommon, unfamiliar diamonds can encounter sensational value floods with even a modest quantity of exposure. A few investors follow a technique of searching out these pearls, yet regularly they end up with all-around run companies that the market doesn't care for. Generally, they are fundamentally acceptable companies with restricted growth potential. Significant investors scan for companies with, for all intents and purposes, boundless growth potential.

Stock Moves: Upward

Why a stock cost is moving upward is generally imperative to investors who don't currently claim it yet might want to be in on the activity. Ordinarily, when there is an abrupt flood in either the stock market or an individual stock, the news shows up rapidly to trumpet the occasion.

When to Buy

Some believe that it is always a good time to buy stocks, because over the long haul, the stocks will develop and succeed. Basically, that is right, although there can clearly be better occasions over others to buy them. Typically, the best time to buy stock, all in all, is the point at which a downtrend turns up and emphatically crosses the trend line. If this is the start of another uptrend and not only an optional trend, but the planning also ought to be acceptable.

THE RULES TO FOLLOW IN THE STOCK MARKET

T he bait of large money has constantly tossed investors into the lap of stock markets. In any case, bringing in money in values isn't simple. It requires gobs of tolerance and control, yet besides, a lot of research and a sound comprehension of the market, among others.

Added to this is the way that stock market instability over the most recent couple of years has left investors in a mess. They are in a quandary whether to invest, hold, or sell in such a situation. Albeit no definite shot equation has yet been found for accomplishment in stock markets, here are some brilliant guidelines which, whenever followed judiciously, may build your odds of getting a decent return:

The stock market is the place the newest understudies at Online Trading Academy are most agreeable when they show up. They have exchanged stocks already, either as individual shares or as parts of a mutual fund bought by their 401(k). They comprehend the idea of owning a bit of an organization and wagering on how well that organization will do in the close to term. These stock market nuts and bolts are entirely agreeable to them.

In any case, your nature with companies recorded on the stock exchanges can really be a disservice. It's enticing, and it can even feel enthusiastic about buying an organization's stock since you like its items or its administration, or because their home office is in your old neighborhood. Stock market nuts and bolts disclose to us that we should search for a solid organization, with great administration, in a growth industry—these are classified as"fundamentals." The issue with the fundamental methodology is that when an organization flashes positive signs for every one of these characteristics, its cost has just expanded to mirror a positive view from the market. Its further upside potential might be restricted, making it really riskier as opposed to a "blue chip" stock to invest in.

Stock Market Basics Rule #1: Focus on Price

Taught traders follow a totally different arrangement of criteria. These traders center around a solitary thought: cost. It might be an ineffectively run organization at the same time, if conditions require a concise improvement in its value, it's a decent buy for the broker who realizes when to get in and when to leap out for a snappy profit. On the other hand, an extraordinary organization will now and again move out of its customary range of familiarity to a cost where, unexpectedly, there are more willing sellers than buyers. This implies cost is going to fall, and it's the short seller who will receive the rewards.

Stock Market Basics Rule #2: Stay Liquid

There are two principal segments to this standard. To begin with, the stock must be effectively exchanged—at any rate, 100,000 shares in day-by-day volume. On the off chance that trading stocks underneath that level, you risk being stuck in a position basically because there are no traders on the opposite side. Second, you should adhere to tickers with a cost beneath $50 essentially because the liquidity necessities over that level become diverting for most traders.

Stock Market Basics Rule #3: Practice Before You Jump In

This is ostensibly the most significant stock market nuts and bolts rule. Instead of investing in the wide market, you ought to think about after a couple of tickers and finding a workable pace trading range well indeed. Keep in mind this is a stock market fundamentals approach that centers on cost. When you know where it "should" exchange, then you'll be very much situated to distinguish a takeoff from the standard and act rapidly for a positive outcome. This is something contrary to "buy and hold" since you may stack up on a stock toward the beginning of the day, dump it toward the evening, or a day or two later, at that point, buy it again when conditions change. It's a skeptical way to deal with the markets in which the most significant thought is your own longing to be fruitful.

Stock Market Basics Rule #4: Don't Try to Out-Think the Markets

Here's a situation you've likely seen: an organization in a division has an awful quarter, or possibly an item review, and all stocks in that area decrease although different companies have done nothing incorrectly. It's silly, yet that is how the market works. So also, fair companies will go up in cost when the market is hot because"a rising tide lifts all pontoons."

At the point when you're centered exclusively around cost—the premise of the protected trading technique instructed at Online Trading Academy—you needn't bother with the markets to be intelligent. You just need to recognize the zones where market interest is probably going to be out of equalization; at that point, buy or sell when value enters these zones. Experience lets us know there are huge amounts of unfilled buy or sell orders at these value levels and, when the requests are filled, the cost will alter course paying, little mind to what else is occurring in the economy or the market.

Different Rules To Follow

Rule 1-Do Not Be "Covetous"

Covetousness in the stock market is never something to be thankful for! On the off chance that, for instance, you purchased a stock at 5, you see that in a brief timeframe increment in value up to 7-8 and didn't start to take profits, and it will be a system that at some point or another will prompt more secure misfortune! Nobody has ever lost money by making profits! All things considered, the goal of the activities of the market is to bring in money, isn't that so? Sometimes, eagerness can make you do a great deal of money at first; however, in the end, you will get just disillusionment. Along these lines, take your profits when you and revalued them again your activities. If you need to prevail in the stock market, endeavor to sell shares when you have profit; at that point, proceed onward to the following deal.

Rule 2-Do Not Buy Stocks in Freefall.

Now and again, this standard is broken because it is anything but difficult to need to buy stocks that are going down. This book will reveal to you that while you may be fortunate sometimes, never buy stocks that are going down because they are as of now doing what you don't need them to do! Oppose the compulsion to buy this sort of activity.

Rule 3-Buy Sharp Increment Activities

The obtaining of shares that are developing is one of the most significant guidelines in the stock market. An activity that is going up is, as of now, doing what you need me to do! To examine the market of the "most sizzling titles" during the arrangement and prepare to play when the opening chime.

Rule 4-Buy Shares in the Best Snapshot of the Day

One of the buying strategies of the best activities that I know is to buy a stock at the hour of day exact, particularly somewhere in the range of 10.00 am and 11.00 am, the point at which the stock will arrive at its "greatest" top. The shares bought in that time and that they arrive at their most extreme day by day will, in general, draw in more buyers because the title is going up. Be careful the bogus breakout (a value move that breaks a help, an opposition, a technical investigation figure).

The perfect circumstance is the point at which a title that opens, for instance, to 3.50 dollars, sells out to 3.10, yet no later than 10:00 am back close to the high of the day and afterward gets through. The volume will increment, and the activity should begin to rise further. Remember, this doesn't generally work. However, the achievement rate is high. It will likewise be critical to have a "stop misfortune."

The system of the stop misfortune request works right now. Essentially it has the means to restrict a potential misfortune (stop loss) of a merchant in that it builds up a span parameter and the limit value (most extreme cost) past which it must sell (or buy on account of a market request). Set forth plainly imparts to value; if the market arrives at a sequential value than the beginning value, the broker will naturally sell or buy. If that is conveyed to the trading programming a value beneath which you need to sell (stop misfortune), the activity or the security is sold quickly, restricting the capital misfortune to 1% or 2%.

The Rule of the Investment: Always Decrease Losses

At the point when you begin trading on the stock market, you have to realize how to control your losses. Your degree of risk chasing or risk repugnance is close to home. In this way, no one can structure misfortune control rules for you. You should do it for yourself:

• Would you loyally follow each buy/sell signal produced by a given marker when the backtest of the pointer predicts that you will have some individual exchanges that involve lost 50%of your trading capital?

• How a lot of your trading capital would you say you are set up to lose? Your answer is basic to whether you prevail in technical trading. If you state, you can acknowledge no losses by any stretch of the imagination, overlook technical trading. You will take losses in technical trading. On the off chance that you state that you're willing to lose 50% in a solitary exchange—hold up, Nellie! That is excessive. After three or four losing exchanges a line, you wouldn't have enough capital left to do any exchanges.

A stop-misfortune request is a request put with a broker to buy or sell once the stock arrives at a specific cost. A stop-misfortune is intended to confine an investor's misfortune to a security position. Setting a stop-misfortune request for 10% underneath the cost at which you purchased the stock will confine your misfortune to 10%.

You will lose money sooner or later on the off chance that you invest in stocks. It will undoubtedly happen eventually. Truth be told, it may have happened as of now, and you didn't understand it since losses can take a few unique structures.

In its least difficult and maybe most excruciating structure, you buy a stock at that point, watch the cost go down, and remain down. Sooner or later, you choose to end the torment and sell it. This kind of misfortune is known as a capital misfortune since it includes a real dollar sum.

You can utilize a capital misfortune to balance profits, called capital additions, for charge purposes. In any case, past that, they're only a difficult investing exercise.

Lost Opportunities

Another kind of misfortune is less excruciating yet, at the same time, genuine. You may have purchased $10,000 of a hot growth stock, and after one year, after some high points and low points, the stock is exceptionally near what you paid for it.

You may be enticed to let yourself know, "Well, at any rate, I didn't lose anything." But that is not valid. You tied up $10,000 of your money for a year, and you didn't get anything consequently. On the off chance that you had purchased a bank CD, it would have earned you, in any event, a smidgen of premium.

Each stock buy starts with an estimation against a without risk investment, for example, a U.S. Treasury note. Ask yourself the amount more would you be able to procure buying a specific stock with some extra risk contrasted with what you could have earned on a note with no risk.

At the point when a stock goes no place or doesn't coordinate the without risk-return of security, you're losing money. You lost the chance to invest your money in something that would have earned you a positive return far beyond the without risk-return—and that is a genuine misfortune.

Missed Profit Losses

This sort of misfortune results when you watch a stock make a critical run-up then fall back, something that can occur with increasingly unstable stocks. Very few individuals are effective at calling the top or base of a market or a stock. You may feel that the money you could have made is lost money—money you would have had on the off chance that you had recently sold at the top.

Numerous investors hold on and trust the stock will "recuperate" and recapture the high, yet that may never occur. Regardless of whether it does, an excessive number of investors hang on seeking after much more noteworthy profits just to see the stock retreat once more. The best solution for this kind of misfortune is to be content with a sensible profit and don't attempt to press each penny out of stock, risking a retreat and a missed profit misfortune.

Paper Losses

You can reveal to yourself that "It's just a paper misfortune," or "If I don't sell, I haven't lost anything," yet the truth is on the off chance that you commit an error or something unanticipated occurs, you need to settle on some solution for it.

On the off chance that you accept the organization's long-haul possibilities are still acceptable, it may be a decent time to add to your possessions. Then again, your paper misfortune turns into a lost chance if you accept this is the place the stock is going to remain, and you sit on that paper misfortune when you could have invested your money in something that procures you a profit.

Managing It

Nobody needs to endure the lossof any sort, yet don't let your sense of self impede settling on the correct choice when it occurs. The best strategy is regularly to cut your losses and proceed onward to the following arrangement. There are different approaches to take a full breath and push ahead, as well.

Survey the choices you made with a virus eye after some time has passed. Would you be able to have done anything any other way? OK, have you lost less or maybe nothing at all on the off chance that you had acted unexpectedly? Attempt to gain from experience.

Fix your money related belt for some time if you should, and if the misfortune is little enough that you can recover it with a little order. Recover that money. At that point, attempt once more, remembering the things you learned for whenever the market gets temperamental.

The Significance of Following the Bearing the Course of the Stock Market/for What Reason Is It Imperative to Follow the Heading of the Stock Market

You might be investing in the best and most brilliant stocks in the market and as yet asking why you are down on your position. Understanding the stock market's heading is basic to any position you take in the market. Battling the trend is a snappy formula for losing your money, regardless of how profitable the organization you are investing in is. Knowing whether you are in a bull market, or you are in the bear market, or a level market is similarly significant and key in surveying the potential for your exchange.

Before starting a long or short position, comprehend the stock market bearing and sign for whether it needs to move sequentially. The ideal approach to do this is to take a gander at an expansive market measure.

Cost and volume study are really the key segments that you have to contemplate. Keep in mind and indicators are largely subsidiaries of these two key segments.

Market Reversal Indicators

Many neglect to act at market tops. At the point when your signs give you a sign that a market top is close by, sell a segment of your long shares out right away. Here are a couple of signs that show an adjustment in the stock market bearing.

Figure out How to Day Trade 7x Faster than Everyone Else

- The Law of Effort versus Result-This key standard is significant for you to observe when you watch it. At the point when markets are at first breaking out, there will be heavier volume than the previous days; in any case, when you start to say that volume is remaining reliably high or in any event, growing,but there is no considerable value in increasing speed, be alert. This is an indication of dissemination and demonstrates that the stock market's heading might be going to turn around. What is this letting you know? General society is exceptionally bullish, and that there is a great deal of buying going on; however, there is likewise a huge power that is keeping the market topped out while they are selling to people in general. The market will, for the most part, go under circulation during development instead of decay. The bigger foundations and speculative stock investments can't sell when every other person is; the huge number of shares that they should sell will make a horrible circumstance for selling overwhelming sizes. They have to cover their selling notwithstanding quality so they can go un-saw and dump their shares. If you discover holding the pack on the underlying sell-off, stay tuned for a bob, which will permit you to sell your shares out.

- The Volume-There is a misnomer that the stock markets need to unmistakably demonstrate overwhelming volume on the drawback to be viewed as a real decrease. This isn't valid. As a general rule, the main decrease off the top will be on lower volume as it isn't yet acknowledged by people in general. On most occasions, you will really observe volume quicken when the open starts to begin tolerating the way that the stock market bearing has really turned lower. The horde mindset will have numerous sellers freezing simultaneously, bringing about the overwhelming volume on a flush lower. The cost, nonetheless, might be extensively off the highs before this occurs.

- Divergences between Market Indices-Keep a nearby eye on this. I will, in general, take a gander at the NYSE to decide the master plan. The issue now and again with the DOW is that it just has 30 stocks in it, and that may show an unexpected picture in comparison to the whole market all in all. Accordingly, watch out for the divergences between the diverse market midpoints to comprehend if a meeting or a decrease in one area or record is conflicting to the general market in general. For instance, if the DJIA is up 1.5% and the NYSE is just up about .5%, we can plainly observe that there is a markup in just a little piece of the market. This can demonstrate that an adjustment in the stock market heading is close.

- Interest Rates-This is a key marker to look too. It straightforward, when the government funds rate and rebate rates are moved higher in progression by the Federal Reserve, a negative stance is taken by the markets. Then again, the top-notch cut that comes after these increments can be believed to end the bear and get the bulls. Likewise, watch out for M1, M2 money supply changes, and the % changes in the Consumer Price Index (CPI).

- Darlings to Dogs-It is average to see a pivot into the slowpokes or canines of the market close to market tops. At the point when you see numerous canines moving higher, observe and notice the sign that you are accepting, which is that the market is preparing for a significant descend.

- January Effect-As talked about in our article on the January impact in the stock markets, a negative close for the long stretch of January is an extremely bearish sign and prompts sizeable market fiascos in the next months.

- Advance/Decline Line-The A/D line quantifies the combined number of stocks progressing as opposed to declining on the NYSE. This pointer isn't exact; recollect that market tops take significantly longer to shape than market bottoms. Voracity is an unexpected creature in comparison to fear as dread hits everybody simultaneously. The A/D line can begin to show divergences far before the market best out; however, it is making an understood articulation in that the market is revitalizing on fewer stocks going higher. While it won't demonstrate the specific top, it will show you ahead of time that the market is starting to sputter and to be careful about a top development being set up.

- AAII Sentiment-AAII measures the opinion of the non-proficient evaluated investment network. It speaks to a proportion of bulls and bears out of the whole populace of those surveyed. This marker happens to centrality when the value of the AAII bull proportion gets beneath 30% bulls. While the events are uncommon, it isn't something to overlook. At the point when the bull proportion is underneath 30%, it means that general society is extremely bearish. This pointer is to be utilized as a contra-marker to the current bearing of the stock market. Bearish readings really are bullish for the market.

- Up/Down Volume on the NYSE-I search for a considerable length of time of solid propelling volume to declining volume after a decay to recommend a progressively significant base may have been placed in. Utilizing a trailing 30 days as a guide, on the off chance that we see three 90% up volume days without a 90% down day on the NYSE, it means that an all the more impressive development in the coming months. While there might be momentary conditions that warrant a pullback, the outline for the following a year is bullish.

- New Highs and New Lows-Another incredible instrument that

quantifies the level of stocks in a record are setting new multi-week highs and lows. It is an oscillator that ranges from 0 to 100. This marker is progressively valuable in finding market bottoms. A perusing underneath 10% demonstrates that we ought to be on.

- VIX Volatility Index-The VIX is inferred utilizing the suggested instability in the S&P 500 record calls and puts. It is a desire for the unpredictability of the market throughout the following 30 days. The higher the instability, the more dread there is in the markets. Once more, this is a contrarian marker, and when this file comes to over 30, utilize your other technical signs and begin searching for an adjustment in the stock markets heading to the upside. During this all-encompassing downturn in the markets, the instability has gone to record levels and has remained that path for a half year as the markets keep on slamming lower. Verifiably 30 is a huge level; notwithstanding, during an emergency, this number can head a lot higher.

- Cycles-While nothing is great, the 4-year cycle in the stock markets is uncanny with its unwavering quality to give significant lows in the stock market. It is truly straightforward; you should search for a low in the stock market like clockwork. How about we think back ever, 2006, 2002, 1998, 1994, 1990, 1986, 1982 all gave astonishing buying openings in the stock market. I said it's not great, and the 1987 accident was one of those events. Because of this lofty drop, the markets founded controls in which closes down the exchanges during extraordinary sell-offs. On the off chance that one had purchased the market in 1986, they would have had the option to make significant gains before the 1987 accident happened. History proposes that we should search for this base in the August to October time span.

The Real-Time to Enter and Leave the Stock Market

Appropriate Time to Enter and Exit the Stock Market

Stock Investment is risky in nature. You can do a vast investigation before stock investment. A lot of investors vouch for fundamental investigation, and others wager for technical examination. The investigation isn't right or wrong. It is significant how it is being done and what is the finish of an investor. A correct investigation with an inappropriate end is on a par with the wrong examination. This post isn't identified with the singular stock investigation as it is a unique ball game by and large.

The stock investment isn't just about carefully selecting singular stocks. An investor additionally needs to measure the expansive/large scale level notions. If you are riding against the feelings, at that point, you will bound to lose. An investor ought to consistently ride with the tide. Failures go against the flow. An investor ought not to be overly hopeful. This is particularly valid for stock investment. I am not saying that stock investment openings are not there during unfriendly occasions.

The Stock Investment – Time to Enter and Exit the Stock Market

As a thumb rule, you ought to enter and exit dependent on the following 4 information focuses, and stock determination is the next basic advance. When you chose to enter the market, then you should search for good stocks accessible around then.

1. The P/E Ratio of NIFTY: P/E proportion for stock investment is the proportion of Market Value to Earning per Share. On the off chance that the P/E is high, that implies the stock is trading at a higher valuation contrasted with gaining. On the off chance that P/E is 24, then it implies as an investor, I will pay Rs 24 for every 1 Rs gaining of the organization. To put it plainly, it is a premium over procuring of the organization. I found an exceptionally solid relationship between the P/E proportion of Nifty with market development. At the point when the P/E of Nifty crosses 24, then the likelihood of downtrend is exceptionally high; for example, valuations are exceptionally rich. Then again, when the P/E of Nifty is beneath 16, then there is a solid chance of upward development. For stock investment, the perception of Nifty P/E is as per the following:

   - More prominent than 24: SELL and EXIT.
   - Between 20 to 24: Be Cautious, and the market may turn restless/unpredictable.

- Between 16 to 20: Buy Cautiously in particular stocks.

- Between 12 to 16: Accumulate.

- Under 12: I will sell my home to invest in the Stock Market.

Under 12 P/E is a profoundly impossible situation: When P/E contacts 24, the likelihood of negative returns is exceptionally HIGH. Incidentally, when the market began a downward trend in March'15, then the NIFTY was trading at a P/E of 24. In this way, effective investors QUIT the market. Presently they are sitting tight for P/E of 16 to enter.

2. The P/B Ratio of NIFTY: For stock investment, P/B proportion is another basic factor. In layman's terms, the Book value of the organization is all out the resource value of the organization. At the end of the day, as indicated by the organization, what is the genuine/genuine value of the organization/stock? For instance, as an organization, my book value is Rs 100; however, the stock is trading at Rs 200. Subsequently, the P/B proportion is 2. So, the stock is overrated. As indicated by the guideline of value investment, you ought to invest in a stock when P/B is 0.8. For example, the stock is underestimated. For all intents and purposes, it is beyond the realm of the imagination at the file level. The current P/B of Nifty is 2.98. We should check from the file point of view.

- More prominent than 4.5: SELL and EXIT.

- Between 3.5 to 4.5: Be Cautious, and the market may turn restless/unpredictable.

- Between 2.75 to 3.5: Buy Cautiously in particular stocks.

- Between 2 to 2.75: Accumulate.

- Under 2: I will sell my home to invest in the Stock Market.

3. Profit Yield of NIFTY: It is the least significant among every one

of the three proportions for stock investment. The explanation being profit is pronounced by just Cash Rich companies. The profit yield is essentially Annual Dividend Per Share separated by Share Price. If the stock cost is Rs 100 and the yearly profit is Rs 2, then the dividend yield is 2%.

- Under 1%: SELL and EXIT

- Between 1% to 2%: Be Cautious, and the market may turn restless/unpredictable.

- Between 2% to 3%: Buy Cautiously in particular stocks.

- Between 3% to 4%: Accumulate

- Above 4%: I will sell my home to invest in the Stock Market.

4. FII's Trading: As a thumb rule, you ought to enter when FII's are buying and leave when they begin selling. The average model is FII buying from Aug'13 till Mar'15. The stock market was ablaze during this period. At the point when FII's begun selling, the markets turned unpredictable. Presently we are in the alarm selling stage.

The focuses partook right now just more extensive indicators. It doesn't ensure positive comes back from stock investment. The individual stock determination is the second critical stage after you choose to enter the market. Any investment choice ought not to be founded on a bunch model. The macroeconomic indicators and drivers of the economy should bolster your choice.

HOW TO MANAGE THE UPPER MARKET TRENDS AND DOWNWARD MARKET TRENDS

Market trends allude to the general development of an investment market. Individuals engaged with stock markets endeavor to recognize the current sort of development that is occurring just as a venture to what extent the current development or trend is probably going to proceed. Figuring out what sort of investments to buy and sell is extraordinarily affected by precisely surveying and anticipating trends.

The way toward distinguishing market trends depends extraordinarily on the idea of a productive market hypothesis. Basically, this idea includes understanding that money related markets supply the structure squares required to settle on the most proficient method to buy and sell since it is conceivable to investigate the components prompting the current market condition. By analyzing proficient market theory, it is conceivable to see how the market is at the current position, which variables are probably going to mold the market, and what circumstances could happen to change the current trend sooner or later.

Generally, investors and brokers will, in general, gathering trends into three classifications. Essential trends are developments that apply to most of the stocks exchanged on the market or inside a particular area of the market. For the most part, an essential trend will proceed for in any event a year and at times longer. Optional trends happen and turn around inside a shorter time span, regularly from two or three weeks to a month or something like that. Toward the start of this kind of trend, it could conceivably be clear if the current trend will stop and turn around for the time being or keep going long enough to be named an essential trend.

Common market trends are not constantly separated from essential trends. However, investors and brokers who acknowledge the thought will, in general, distinguish it as an essential trend that has proceeded for at least five years. It isn't incredible for a trend of this sort to proceed for up to 25 years.

Notwithstanding current market trends, it is conceivable to settle on investing choices that make a sensible return. The key is to recognize the current trend that commands the stock market, precisely venture to what extent it will last, and position investments in a way that will, in the long run, yield an attractive measure of revenue. By picking the correct stocks at the opportune time, it is conceivable to brave a downward trend with almost no misfortune in the value of the investment portfolio and be in a perfect situation to make a lot of money once the market starts to move upward.

HOW TO BUY STOCKS

Despite the higher-than-normal instability, when you buy stock and gain the legitimate option to take an interest in the profits and losses of the undertaking, your money can develop suchthat it is justpreposterous with securities, authentications of the store, or at times, even land. For new investors and would-be investors, one of the more typical inquiries posed includes how to buy the stock the mechanics of really getting your hands on that bit of proprietorship qualifying you for dividends that are immediately stored or sent to your family so you can appreciate the surge of passive income.

There are a few distinct approaches to buy stock, each with its own focal points and hindrances, including assessment and liquidity contemplations. Some well-known options can assist you with increasing the general format of the land and be better educated to settle on choices of value securing.

The Most Effective Method to Buy Stock in aRegular, Taxable Brokerage Account

If you need to buy stock without any limitations, no favorable duty circumstances and no commitment restrains, the most effortless route is to open a brokerage account. Picking a particular brokerage house includes a few contemplations, for example, regardless of whether you need a full-administration broker or a rebate broker that does simply executing your stock exchanges at absolute bottom costs, however nowadays, it is as simple as taking five minutes to round out a progression of inquiries on the web.

Envision you needed to open a record at Charles Schwab and Company, probably the greatest broker in the United States. You would round out the online application, giving your name, address, government disability number, work data, and all the more, relying on whether you needed to include edge obligation capacity or stock option trading benefits. You would then send in the base record equalization of $1,000 or, on the other hand, pursue $100 every month direct stores or electronic scopes from Schwab financial records.

When your brokerage account had been opened, you would see the money stored and stopped, hanging tight for you to accomplish something with it. You would sign on to the site, enter the ticker image of the organization you needed to buy, enter the number of shares you needed to buy, and present the exchange a couple of snaps once you had checked the subtleties. By and large, inside a second or two, you'd see the stock saved into your record and the money pulled back. A couple of days after the fact, you'd get an exchange affirmation archive.

At whatever point the organization delivered a profit, you'd see it direct stored into your brokerage account. On the off chance that the organization at any point had a tax-exempt side project or split-off, you'd see those shares saved into your brokerage account, also (e.g., Chipotle Mexican Grill was separated from McDonald's while Allstate Insurance was spun-off from Sears). The most effective method to Buy Stock in a Roth IRA, Traditional IRA, SIMPLE IRA, SEP-IRA, or Other Similar Retirement Account

From the point of a stray piece of view, the way toward buying stock in a Roth IRA or any of its related cousins is for all intents and purposes indistinguishable from buying stock in a standard, assessable brokerage account. If your IRA is held at a brokerage firm, you follow precisely the same methodology. The distinction has to do with how the charges are dealt with and the measure of new money you can contribute every year.

For instance, you can possibly contribute $5,500 to a Traditional IRA if you are 49 years of age or more youthful, and $6,500 on the off chance that you are 50 years old or more established. For whatever length of time that you fall beneath as far as possible as a result for the year dependent on your conjugal status, you can discount these commitments as though you never brought in the money. In the interim, the dividends and capital pick up your money gains while investing in stock inside the Traditional IRA are totally tax-exempt with just a bunch of special cases. At the point when you go to haul the money out of the record, you pay a customary income charge on the sum pulled back.

If you attempt to pull back the money too soon, you'll be dependent upon a 10% punishment charge except if you meet one of the eight exclusions. The most effective method to Buy Stock through a Direct Stock Purchase Plan or Dividend Reinvestment Plan (otherwise known as DRIP).

Imagine a scenario where you would prefer not to open a brokerage account. You're in karma. Numerous companies (particularly enormous blue-chip shares) support programs that permit you to buy stock straightforwardly from the company's exchange specialist for free or at a financed cost. Consider the advanced relative of John D. Rockefeller's oil realm, Exxon Mobil. It supports an immediate stock buy plan through a business called Computershare. Would-be proprietors who open a record with either $250 or consent to having $50 every month pulled back from a checking or bank account can buy the stock at no commission. Surprisingly better, the arrangement permits partial stock buys, so every penny gets set to work for you, the investor, regardless of whether you don't have precisely the perfect add up to obtain a full offer at some random time.

At the point when you apply on the web, you can tell the exchange specialist whether you need your dividends direct saved into your checking or bank account or reinvested in extra shares of stock. Choose cautiously. While there is no set-in-stone answer—everything relies upon your own budgetary circumstance and the resulting execution of the stock itself—there is a major contrast between reinvesting and not reinvesting your dividends over extensive stretches of time in case you're lucky enough to wind up possessing a really extraordinary endeavor.

Step-by-Step Instructions to Buy Stock Through an Employee Stock Purchase Plan

One of the greatest neglected advantages in corporate America, a ton of enormous companies permit representatives to turn into a proprietor of the firm at appealing limits, frequently as high as 15% off the stock market cost, through projects known as Employee Stock Purchase Plans. Truth be told, some scholarly research shows the average representative surrenders somewhere in the range of $4,000 and $5,000 in free money every year by not exploiting ESPPs they are qualified to join.

Much of the time, you have to go down to the HR division and request an enlistment structure. You tell the organization the amount of your check you need to be retained to buy shares. Each payroll interval, some portion of the money you would have earned is, rather, used to buy a stock at a less expensive cost than you could have paid through a brokerage firm (e.g., for an organization with a 15% markdown, a $100 stock would be offered to you for $85, giving you a moment $15 profit).

Step-by-Step Instructions to Buy Stock Through a Mutual Fund

On the off chance that you would prefer not to pick singular stocks, however, need to possess stocks in any case, your most solid option is a mutual fund; in all likelihood, an ease record fund. To put it plainly, you compose a check or have the underlying sum removed from your financial balance, so your money is pooled with different investors. The fund chiefs at that point utilize the money to go out and buy stocks for your sake, holding them in a brought together, a combined portfolio that is, itself, partitioned into shares that you possess. Notwithstanding a commission, which you may need to pay, you in a roundabout way pay a lot of the fund's cost, which is communicated as the mutual fund cost proportion.

We should envision you needed to buy an S&P 500 record found. You would open a record straightforwardly with the mutual fund organization, or you could have your stockbroker buy shares through your brokerage account, the last of whom may charge you a commission on the shares while the mutual fund organization doesn't for in-house funds. The fund distributes investor money to stocks dependent on something known as market capitalization. The best ten stocks, as a gathering, get 17.8% of your money.

At whatever point you buy extra shares of your mutual fund by sending another check or having an electronic exchange transaction using your financial balance, just as when you have mutual fund disseminations (made up of capital increases and dividends as a rule) consequently reinvested into the fund, you are in a roundabout way buying stocks.

The shares you possess of huge organizations are just as genuine as though you held them legitimately in your brokerage account; there is only a lawful mediator between you that offers economies of scale and broadening.

The Most Effective Method to Buy Stock Through a 401(k) Plan

Except if you have a self-coordinated 401(k) at a brokerage firm, you are certainly must browse a record of mutual funds picked by your boss to get the presentation to stocks, buying in a roundabout way as though you were buying a mutual fund all alone. The human asset office can assist you with setting up your record, get a lot of the free coordinating money that could conceivably be offered, and ensure commitments are distributed to the funds you think best fits your needs.

Most fair 401(k) plans will offer in any event a huge capitalization stock fund, a little capitalization stock fund, and a universal stock fund for the individuals who need to claim global (non-U.S. companies) that deliver dividends in numerous monetary standards. On the off chance that your 401(k) plan offered the Vanguard Total International Stock Index Fund, by method for delineation, the best 10 possessions would speak to 8.3% of your benefits.

Remember Nestle for Switzerland, Royal Dutch Shell in the United Kingdom, Novartis in Switzerland, Roche Holding in Switzerland, HSBC in the United Kingdom, Toyota Motor in Japan, Samsung Electronics in South Korea, BHP Billiton in Australia, BP in the United Kingdom, and Bayer in Germany. At the point when you settled on this fund on your 401(k) assignment guidelines, you are buying stocks in these organizations, to say the very least.

The Most Effective Method to Buy Stock in an International Company

Imagine a scenario in which you are an investor in the United States who needs to buy shares of an organization headquartered in someplace outside of the nation. There are a couple of various ways for you to do this, practically, which are all going to experience your brokerage account.

- If the remote stock has a posting on an American stock exchange, for example, the New York Stock Exchange, you can buy shares by entering the ticker image similarly as you would some other household business. English liquor goliath Diageo PLC, for instance, exchanges under ticker image DEO in the United States.
- If the remote stock has American Depository Receipts and American Depository Shares that have been made, you can buy these in the United States through the ADS ticker image. This is a perplexing point that would require its own inside and out clarification and is presumably not suitable for most new investors, given the cash risks included and outside retention assessed that might be expected. A model would be Nestle, which exchanges the pink sheets in the United States under the image NSRGY. Those are actually a kind of trust fund that holds the real Nestle shares over in Zurich, Switzerland, helpfully set up by Citibank for American investors.
- You can open a unique kind of brokerage account that offers worldwide trading abilities. Many significant brokers have this administration. The worldwide trading record will hold different cash adjusts just as shares of stock bought legitimately on outside stock markets; however, will cost significantly more with commissions now and again running as high as a few hundred dollars and least buys frequently being set at a huge number of American proportional dollars per exchange.
- You can pick to buy a household mutual fund that centers around global stocks like the one recently depicted in the 401(k) segment.

A Few Closing Thoughts on How to Buy Stock

There are a bunch of different approaches to buy stock, including setting up a family association through something like a constrained risk organization or, in any event, discovering somebody who claims shares, haggling straightforwardly, and moving the stock between yourselves bypassing the stock exchanges altogether.

However, there is practically no condition under which a standard, a non-control investor could ever think that it's important to do something like this except if the individual was moving shares of stock to a youngster, grandkid, or beneficiary at a limited cost for the different expense and legacy reasons that are long ways past the extent of this conversation.

Get the job done it to state, how you buy your stock can have gigantic ramifications for your primary concern profits. However, by and large, you will do practically the entirety of your buys through a stockbroker, a mutual fund organization, or a business supported retirement plan, for example, 401(k) or 403(b).

The large key to progress is to discover acceptable, quality companies, follow through on a sensible cost (or if you don't have the foggiest idea how to do that, dollar cost normal), and afterward, do what affluent families do by shunning portfolio turnover. This will permit you to maintain a strategic distance from frictional costs as well as exploit conceded charge resources now and again, which can add a few rates that focus on your aggravating rate.

The Unstable Earnings and Deal Growth

For some business visionaries, propelling another business regularly implies strolling a scarcely discernible difference between seeking after earnings growth and developing the top-line revenue.

A business can't be fruitful in the long haul without winning a profit. However, it likewise should reinvest a portion of its profit to develop past a startup, venturing into new markets or topographical regions.

Understanding the contrasts between earnings growth versus revenue growth will help entrepreneurs organize their next growth steps and to perceive the distinction between expanding profitability versus expanding deals volume.

Earnings

Understanding the contrast between "earnings" and "revenue" is basic to understanding the contrasts between earnings growth versus revenue growth. The expression "earnings" is basically characterized as the net profit earned from the activities of a business or the measure of money left over after the business has paid all expenses related to working the business.

When figuring earnings growth, it is significant not to incorporate one-time occasions, for example, the offer of benefits, premium income or costs, claim grants, and so on. Such income and costs are non-working or fund related occasions. Earnings growth is estimated from business working income, not business overall gain.

Earnings Growth Rate Formula

The revenue growth rate equation is as per the following:

- Earnings Growth Rate = {Total Earnings for a period fewer Earnings for past period/Total Earnings Growth for Prior Period} x 100
- For model: If the Net Earnings in Year 2 and Year 1 was $480,000 and $400,000, individually, at that point Earnings Growth Rate in year 2 would be: $480,000 – $400,000 = $80,000 and $80,000/$400,000 = .20 X 100 = 20 Percent Earnings Growth Rate.

Revenue

Then again, "revenue" is characterized as gross income, or the aggregate sum of money got for the offer of merchandise and ventures before any costs are deducted. Know that revenue can be deceiving as it applies to profitability since it doesn't consider any business liabilities and immediate or backhanded costs related to the business.

Revenue Growth Rate Formula

The revenue growth rate equation is as per the following:

- Revenue Growth Rate = {Total Revenue for a Period Short Total Revenue for Prior Period} x 100
- For model: If the Gross Revenue in Year 2 and Year 1 was $4,800,000 and $4,000,000, separately, at that point Revenue Growth Rate in year 2 would be: $4,800,000 – $4,000,000 = $800,000 and $800,000/$4,000,000 = .20 X 100 = 20 Percent Revenue Growth Rate.

Earnings Growth versus Revenue Growth

When we have a decent comprehension of earnings and revenue, we can investigate how earnings growth and revenue growth are significant indicators of how monetarily solid a business might be.Commonly, earnings growth alludes to the yearly pace of earnings growth because of investments of money related to capital as money, stock fixed gear, genuine property, and HR (finance).

Investors frequently utilize normal earnings growth to decide if a business is deserving of the investment. As a rule, the more prominent the earnings growth, the better! Earnings are seemingly the most significant estimation of growth for a business, as earnings growth shows the wellbeing and profitability of a business after all costs are paid.

Then again, revenue growth alludes to the yearly growth pace of revenue from all-out deals. The revenue growth metric is significant because it gives a sign of the strength of a business' deals, and all things considered, revenue growth stays a mainstream technique for evaluating how effectively a business is at selling its own items and additionally benefits.

At the point when the revenue for a business is developing consistently and developing at an expanding rate year-over-year, it is an awesome sign of a monetarily solid business. Such a business will be exceptionally appealing when the time has come to sell the business.

It is imperative to remember that (main concern) earnings are, to some degree, reliant on revenue growth. If earnings are relied upon to increment after some time, at that point, it will be almost difficult to do, so except if revenue increments also. At the end of the day, decreasing costs by reducing pointless expenses and making operational efficiencies will just go so far in improving an organization's earnings. To accomplish positive earnings growth after some time, revenue growth will likewise be important.

- Earnings and deals growth.
- A solid profit for value.
- A quickly developing and industry-driving item or administration solid interest among mutual fund administrators.

Stock Market Key Pointer and The Relative Quality

The Relative Strength or RS isn't really a pointer, so in this manner is regularly neglected. It looks at stock or some other instrument to another stock/instrument, and most usually, we analyze, for instance, a stock to a market record, for example, SP-500. Try not to mistake this apparatus for Relative Strength Index-RSI, which is a totally extraordinary marker. (See our page on RSI)

Marker Explained in Detail

You basically partition the stock cost with SP-500 cost, and you get a number utilized for plotting a diagram underneath the stock. Relative Strength-RS can be determined and utilized on whenever outline, from intraday to month-to-month charts, and this figuring depends on shutting value activity.

At the point when the RS is dropping, it implies that the stock is genuinely powerless contrasted with SP-500, and when RS is climbing, the stock is generally solid contrasted with SP-500. Try not to befuddle a falling RS with a falling stock cost. You can, without much of a stretch, have a rising stock with a falling RS, yet it just implies that the stock is climbing reasonably, not exactly SP-500.

There are Four Scenarios When Using RS:

- Price ↑ + RS ↓ = Stock ascensions not exactly SP-500.
- Price ↑ + RS ↑ = Stock ascensions more than SP-500.
- Price ↓ + RS ↑ = Stock drops not exactly SP-500.
- Price ↓ + RS ↓ = Stock drops more than SP-500.

You can utilize any technical pointer and chart investigation on the RS, for example, a moving average or twofold top/twofold base.

RS can surrender your heads on fast change in the value, which is fundamental explanation traders use RS. Another explanation is that traders incline toward buying pioneers in the market, so buying a stock that shows relative quality bodes well. There is no motivation to buy a slacking stock, which is just going up because the market is hauling it up.

Tips and Ideas

There are different employments of RS in trading. The principal use is for passages:

1. When utilizing RS for passages, a smart thought is to search for difference as this is when value makes a higher high; however, the

RS makes a lower high. This gives the merchant additional proof when going short. Search for your sign realizing that the stock is relatively powerless as a section could be a twofold top (with a slightly higher high). The RS has just revealed to us that it doesn't bolster the new high.

2. Another way of utilizing RS for sections is to utilize it for the examination of your entrances. Search for a relatively solid stock and an uptrend in that stock. This discloses to you that it is climbing quicker than, for instance, SP-500, and this builds the chances for your long section.

Utilizing Relative Strength for high chances exchanges

This Indicator is additionally an incredible device revenue-driven taking:

1. Divergence can likewise be utilized in revenue-driven taking. At the point when the stock makes a higher high, and relative quality makes a lower high, then it flags that the stock is never again more grounded than the market, and profit-taking is an insightful decision.

2. As clarified before, numerous traders add indicators to RS. By adding two moving midpoints to your RS, you get an incredible instrument of revenue-driven taking. If you are in exchange and your shorter-term moving normal is crossing down through your more extended term moving normal, then the time has come to take the profit. It implies that your stock is performing more regrettable than the market.

HOW TO BUY SHARES

How to Discover and Assess the Best Protections to Buy and Watch

A large portion of us have known about stocks and shares; however, they don't have a clue about how to buy shares or how to buy stocks. We clarify the way toward investing in shares and stocks right now.

Keep perusing to become familiar with shares, why investing may work out, and why it may not, and how to get your head around the expenses encompassing shares.

What Are Shares?

Otherwise called values and offer speaks to a portion of possession in an organization, and these shares are recorded on a stock exchange. At the point when you discover an offer to buy, you are buying a little stake in an organization. You become a joint-proprietor of the organization alongside the various investors, and you are welcome to have a state in some of the choices the organization makes.

When hoping to buy shares, the point is for the shares to develop in value after some time; furthermore, to profit by an offer in the profits of the organization as standard profit installments. Shares give investors the open door for consistent income and capital growth, albeit neither of these is ensured.

Why Invest in Stocks and Shares?

Verifiably, over the more extended term, which is viewed as in any event ten years, shares have commonly been a superior performing resource than numerous different types of investment, for example, money and securities.Nonetheless, monetary specialists will consistently call attention to that past presentation isn't really a pointer of how well an advantage will act later on.

What Are the Risks of Buying Stocks and Shares?

Offer costs can vacillate out of nowhere, and at times strongly, which is why shares are viewed as a higher-risk investment than money, securities, and property. It's also the motivation behind why they're progressively appropriate as a more drawn-out term investment-on the off chance that you invest over a more extended period. You're in a superior situation to brave any variances in the market. Not all offer investments convey an equivalent risk; the degree of risk relies upon the organization you are hoping to buy shares in.

A little beginning up with a creative item will have a higher risk profile than a blue-chip organization. For example, however, the fascination of the little beginning up is that it might offer the potential for better yields. Likewise, the little beginning up may not deliver out dividends-it might need to reinvest any profits back in the organization, while the bigger, progressively settled company may offer alluring profit payouts.

It's indispensable to explain your investment objectives and risk profile before buying stocks and shares. It's critical to look into any companies you mean to buy shares in to guarantee they offer a reasonable investment open door for you.

The value of shares may increment as organization profits increment or because of market desire, yet the inverse is additionally valid. The value of an offer may fall, and if an organization breakdown, you may lose the entirety of your unique investment. The risk of this incident relies upon the profile of the specific organization you need to invest in. However, there is no sureness about the result of an investment in shares, not at all like a fixed-premium store where you are sure of recovering your capital and procuring a fixed pace of premium.

How Would I Buy Shares?

Regardless of whether you see how shares work, you may at present be asking yourself, 'how would I buy shares?' You can discover shares to buy legitimately from a stockbroker or dealer, or you can buy shares through an investment fund. An investment fund pools your money with different investors, and it likewise invests in shares in the stock of numerous companies.

Since a fund has worked in broadening, the risk is spread and is along these lines, for the most part, lower than buying shares in a solitary organization. You can likewise pick a fund that coordinates your risk profile, yet an investment of this sort isn't without risk-you're despite everything presented to the risk of the stock market falling in value.

HOW TO SELL STOCKS

T he way toward selling a stock is fundamentally the same as buying one: Choosing the correct request type is vital.

Three Stages of Selling Stocks

1. Check Your Feelings

There are valid justifications to sell stocks and awful reasons.

Continuous horrible showing comparative with the challenge, untrustworthy initiative, and the board choices you don't support may all make the rundown of valid justifications. Possibly you've chosen your money would improve somewhere else, or you're reaping losses to counterbalance gains for which you'll owe income charges.

Terrible reasons normally include an automatic response to transient market changes or coincidental organization news. Bailing when things get rough just secures your losses, which is something contrary to what you need. Before you sell a stock, go over you're thinking to guarantee you're not yielding to a passionate reaction you may later lament.

2. Settle on a Request Type

In case you're comfortable with buying stock, you're acquainted with selling it—the options for request types are the equivalent. The objective, be that as it may, is extraordinary: You use request types to restrain costs on the acquisition of stock. On the deal, your principal objective is to restrict losses and expand returns.

Market request: A solicitation to buy or sell a stock ASAP at the best accessible cost. Use it ifyou need to empty the stock at any cost.

Breaking point request: A solicitation to buy or sell a stock just at a particular cost or better. Use it in case you're fine with keeping the stock if you can't sell at or over the value you need.

Stop (or stop-misfortune) request: A market request that is executed just if the stock arrives at the cost you've set. Use it on the off chance that you need to sell if a stock drops to or underneath a specific cost.

Stop-limit request: A blend of a stop request and a breaking point request: An utmost request is executed if your stock drops to the stop cost, however, just on the off chance that you can sell at or over your farthest point cost. Use it ifyou need to sell if a stock drops to a specific cost, however just if you can sell for a base sum.

3.   Round out the Exchange Ticket

Accepting that you're selling through a broker, the broker's site or trading stage will have an exchange ticket or request you'll have to round out to start the deal. As a rule, and at most brokers, the exchange will settle—which means the money from the deal will land in your record—two business days after the date the request executes.

Rounding out the exchange ticket is a snappy procedure: You'll select sell, plug in the image of the stock, the number of shares, your request type (and farthest point or stop cost, if relevant), and what's known as the "time in power" or request termination: basically, to what extent the request ought to stay open.

Your decisions for time-in-power rely upon request type, yet regular options are:

• Day: The exchange will drop, and the request terminates if not filled by market close. This is commonly the default.

• Good-till-canceled: The exchange stays dynamic until filled or dropped;

however, brokers normally limit to what extent investors can leave a GTC request open.

• Immediate or drop: A request that must be filled promptly; in any case, the requestor any segment of it that isn't filled will be dropped.

• Fill or execute: Typically utilized when trading countless shares. If the whole request isn't filled quickly, the exchange will be dropped.

• On the open: Fills at the market's opening cost.

• On the nearby: Fills at the market's end cost.

By and large, it's fine to leave the default day choice set up here. As you get progressively OK with stock trading, you can begin to investigate your options.

The Strong Arrangements of Rules for Selling Stocks

1. Know When to Sell

Realizing when to sell a stock is as significant as realizing when to buy, and both of these activities are administered by energy. You know, at this point, we measure a stock's force by its relative execution (RP) line, which graphically portrays how a stock has performed compared with a market record. As we continued looking for profits, obviously, we scan for stocks that have an up-slanting RP line, which means they're outflanking the market in general.

Since trends will, in general, remain; as a result, stocks with positive RP lines, for the most part, proceed with higher, and the other way around. Hence, we use RP lines not exclusively to recognize potential buys yet to distinguish potential deals also. At the point when a stock's energy turns negative, the chances are that the recently settled downtrend will probably persevere. That demonstrates that it's an ideal opportunity to proceed onward.

The stunt is selling stock after you have allowed them to continue progressing. Following the RP line will never get you out of stock right at the top; it will keep you in solid situations as long as they are solid, getting you out once the odds of a continued development are little.

At Cabot, we have a few standards we use to decide if to sell a stock. Consistently, Cabot editors meet and check the RP lines of the stocks we follow in our growth distributions—Cabot Growth Investor, Cabot Top Ten Trader, and Cabot Global Stocks Explorer—to check whether they've defied any of these guidelines. In the event that they have, out they go! On the off chance that you painstakingly peruse and comprehend these standards, you'll be searching for precisely the same things we do, and you'll know when we discover them.

2.　Momentum Turning Down for Eight Weeks

If things are on track with your organization and its stock and discernment hasn't been forcefully harmed, at that point, a stock's RP line ought to once in a while pull back for over about two months. If a stock's RP line amendment protracts to 10, 12, or 15 weeks, it's most likely revealed to you that the fundamentals of the organization might be changing for more awful because of poor deals or winning, deceleration of growth, and so on. At the point when you see an eight-week amendment, hurl the wellbeing nets and ensure your stock doesn't fall a lot further.

Here are how to do that. Recall that an RP line revision is checked from the ongoing top to another redress low. So, on the off chance that the RP line bottomed a month after it topped, at that point moved sideways for three weeks, that isn't an eight-week adjustment. Just if the RP line hits another adjustment low two months after its pinnacle, it has met the paradigm of an eight-week redress.

Next, take a gander at the value chart and set a psychological stop marginally underneath its current cost, ideally at a region of help. If the stock closes underneath this point quickly, you should sell. Mental stops let you cling to a stock with a slacking RP line as long as the cost is as yet acknowledging, not deteriorating.

3.　30-Degree Rule

This remarkable guideline was created following quite a while of watching, drawing and investigating RP lines. We saw that after a stock had a significant amendment of in any event a month, at that point bounced back unequivocally for about fourteen days; it entered a basic crossroads.

As of now, after a redress and short meeting, a stock's sure energy comes into question. Numerous stocks keep on progressing unequivocally, getting through their old RP highs. Others saw their conventions waver, and they lost their positive energy. How might you tell what direction your stock will go?

We found that, following the underlying fourteen-day rally, if the stock's RP line can remain over a 30-degree upward-slanting trend line drawn from its RP low, at that point, hanging on is your most astute course. On the other hand, if the stock's RP line separates beneath this trend line, the positive energy has blurred, and the stock will probably proceed with its plunge.

Investigations of our portfolio activities have demonstrated that selling stock dependent on the breakdown of the 30-degree line is our top-of-the-line rule. We accept this is because the best time to sell a wavering growth stock is the point at which an assembly following a revision vacillates. Furthermore, that is actually what the 30-degree rule permits you to do!

4.   Two RP Tools That Can Help You Sell Right

Cabot Growth Investor's standards to sell after a 10% to 20% downturn, the eight-week force breakdown, and the 30-degree line infiltration make up our three authority rules for selling. There are, nonetheless, a few instruments we use to assist us with distinguishing inconvenience before it happens. We'd prefer to share those with you also.

To begin with, we're generally vigilant for twofold or triple RP tops. Similarly, as it very well may be a tip-off of shortcoming when a stock makes some intense memories overcoming a given value level, so it does with RP levels. Frequently, when a stock's RP line endeavors to get over a specific point a few times and falls flat, its run is finished, and lower costs can be normal.

The second thing we search for is a disparity between the cost and the RP line. This is an indication that the sponsorship behind the stock is winding down—the buying power that recently caused the stock to beat the general market has since died down, making only a normal market entertainer. This unpretentious decline in sponsorship regularly proceeds until it's not all that inconspicuous! That implies lower costs ahead.

Giving careful consideration to RP lines and setting mental stops will enable you to realize when to sell a stock and take those profits. You will have the option to clutch your solid stocks, enduring their redresses in continuous development. In any case, you will realize when to sell the stocks that disrupt the norms and stay away from large losses.

THE ESSENTIAL STOCK MARKET SALES RULES

The Offensive Standards to Square Profits and the Defensive Guidelines to Lessens Losses

Defensive Stock

A defensive-stock is a stock that gives consistent profit and stable earnings paying little heed to the general stock market condition. Due to the consistent interest for their items, defensive stocks will remain in general stay stable during the different periods of the business cycle. A defensive stock ought not to be mistaken for a "protection stock," which alludes to stock in companies that make things like weapons, ammo, and warrior planes.

Defensive Stock Explained

Defensive stocks will, in general, perform superior to the more extensive market during downturns. Be that as it may, during a development stage, they will, in general, perform underneath the market. This is credited to their low beta or relative risk and execution in the market. Defensive stocks normally have betas of under 1. To show this wonder, think about a stock with a beta of 0.5. On the off chance that the market is relied upon to drop 15%, and the current without risk rate is 3%, a defensive stock will just drop 9% [0.5 x (15%–3%)]. Then again, if the market is relied upon to increment 15%, with a without risk pace of 3%, a defensive stock will just increment 6% [0.5 x (15%–%)].

Investors will participate in general investment in low-beta, defensive stocks if a market downturn is normal. Be that as it may, if the market is relied upon to succeed, dynamic investors will regularly pick stocks with higher betas trying to augment return.

Instances of Defensive Stocks

Defensive stocks are otherwise called "non-repetitive stocks" since they are not profoundly corresponded with the business cycle. The following are a couple of kinds of defensive stocks.

Utilities

Water, gas, and electric utilities are a case of defensive stocks since individuals need them during all periods of the business cycle. Service companies likewise are thought of as profiting by more slow financial conditions since loan fees will, in general, be lower, and their opposition to obtain funds is substantially less.

Buyer Staples

Companies that deliver or circulate customer staples, which are products individuals will, in general, buy out of need paying little mind to monetary conditions, are commonly thought to be defensive. They incorporate nourishment, refreshments, cleanliness items, tobacco, and certain family unit things. These companies produce consistent income and unsurprising earnings during solid and feeble economies. All things considered, their stocks will go, in general, beat non-defensive or buyer repeating stocks that sell optional items during feeble economies while failing to meet expectations in solid economies.

Social insurance Stocks

Shares of significant pharmaceutical companies and clinical gadget producers have verifiably been viewed as defensive stocks, as there will consistently be wiped out individuals needing care. In any case, an expanded challenge from new marked and conventional medications, and vulnerability encompassing medication value guideline, implies they aren't as defensive as they used to be.

Loft REITs

Loft land investment trusts (REITs) are additionally regarded as defensive, as individuals consistently need cover. Besides, REITs are required to pay at least 90% of their assessable income as investor dividends every year. When searching for defensive plays, avoid REITs that emphasize ultra-top of the line lofts; however, just as a place of business REITs or mechanical park REITs, which could see defaults on leases rise when business eases back.

The Role of Defensive Stocks in a Portfolio

Investors trying to ensure their portfolios during a debilitating economy or times of high instability may expand their introduction to defensive stocks. Settled companies, for example, Procter and Gamble, Johnson and Johnson, Philip Morris International, and Coca-Cola, are viewed as defensive stocks. Notwithstanding solid incomes, these companies have solid activities with the capacity to climate debilitating monetary conditions. They additionally deliver dividends, which can have the impact of adding a stock's cost during a market decrease.

Some may ask, "If times are hard or if things are getting unsteady, for what reason would anybody even need to claim a stock? Why not simply go for the wellbeing of a Treasury charge, which basically has a without risk pace of return?" The appropriate response is essentially that dread and insatiability can frequently drive the markets. Defensive stocks oblige eagerness by offering a higher profit yield than can be made in low-financing cost situations. They additionally reduce dread since they are not as risky as standard stocks, and it ordinarily takes a significant disaster to crash their plan of action. Likewise, it ought to be realized that most investment chiefs must choose the option to claim stocks, and if they think times will be more diligently than typical, they will move toward defensive stocks.

SELLING SHARES

An offer is basically a split unit of the value of an organization. Companies issue shares to fund-raise and investors (that is, you) buy shares in organizations since they accept the organization will progress admirably, and they need to 'share' in its prosperity.

Investing in the stock market is a decent way to develop your riches long haul; however, for newcomers, buying and selling shares may appear to be overwhelming. So here is our manual for beginning in the stock market and turning into a more intelligent investor regardless of whether you as of now buy and hold shares.

Why Are Shares Extraordinary?

At the point when you buy shares, you become a fractional proprietor of the organization. While this may appear glaringly evident, it makes share buying fundamentally not the same as bank accounts or, in any event, buying securities.

Investors are not loaning the organization money and, nor are they clients of the organization—they are the organization.

Critically, this implies the value of your investment ascends as the value of the organization ascends on the market. It likewise acquires an offer, any profits that may be conveyed through dividends. Frequently overlooked is that being an investor likewise brings some force and duties.

As an investor, you reserve the privilege to decide on key choices, including executives' compensation, at the yearly gathering or on specific issues like takeovers when they emerge.

The Intensity of Dividends

Dividends are installments made to investors from an organization's profits. However, even profitable organizations don't need to deliver dividends. The executives may choose to save some trade out of the firm for development.

English organization dividends are commonly paid two times every year, and investors can either take the money or decide to utilize the money to buy more shares in the organization.

A few investors buy shares in companies that regularly deliver high dividends to make an income, regardless of whether they don't anticipate that the shares should rise quickly in value.

Reinvesting dividends in shares can drastically build returns over the more drawn-out term just insofar as the shares go up.

Would It Be Advisable for Me to Adhere to Shares that Cost Less?

A few shares can cost under 1p each, while others can cost more than £50. Be that as it may, low-estimated shares are not really better value. Actually, companies whose shares cost only a couple of pence are regularly engaged with risky ventures, for example, mining investigation or innovation. What makes a difference most is whether you accept a firm will progress admirably.

If you need to value shares, at that point, you have to do so utilizing one of the normal valuation techniques. The most usually utilized is the cost-to-earnings proportion or P/E. This thinks about an organization's offer cost to the profits it makes per share.

An organization with a P/E of 10 is being valued at a lower level than an organization with a P/E of 20. This perhaps because it is decided to have poor growth possibilities or because the market has neglected it. Continuously contrast share valuations with the sort of organization that it is, its friends, and the market overall.

What Causes Shares to Go up or down?

Over the long haul, the absolute most significant factor is rising profits or the desire for them. A few different components impact cost. However, on the off chance that the general stock market is rising, numerous shares will be hauled up afterward, and if stockbrokers are idealistic about a specific segment—property, for instance—at that point, shares in companies in the property division will profit.

Recollect that the market takes a gander at the future, not the past, so brokers and huge investors are unquestionably increasingly intrigued by how an organization is relied upon to do in the years ahead than how it performed a year ago.

The assumption is a key driver with regards to share costs. If the market doesn't care for an organization out of the blue, its offer cost can stay discouraged even as it keeps on developing profits. Interestingly, the market may have concluded that it adores an organization—these are regularly called story stocks—and rate it more profoundly than you would anticipate. These inconsistencies in valuation can give chances to investors.

How Would I Buy and Sell Shares?

At the point when an organization first buoys on the stock market, for example, Royal Mail did, it is, in some cases, conceivable to apply for shares straightforwardly from that firm. This is known as an Initial Public Offering (IPO). By and large, in any case, shares are purchased through a stockbroker or a monetary administration firm.

A large number of these organizations permit investors to buy and sell shares online just by rounding out an online structure. Investors can likewise buy and sell shares via telephone by ringing a stockbroker or a money related counselor.

The best wager for a DIY investor is one of the many investing stages accessible, running from those that offer funds just to those that permit you to invest across shares, funds, investment trusts, securities, and that's only the tip of the iceberg.

These will permit you to set up a record on the web and afterward pay in a single amount to invest how you pick or pursue standard direct charge regularly scheduled installments into a choice of investments—or do both.

Most stages are extremely easy to utilize and simple to become acclimated to. They will offer fluctuating degrees of tips, examination, apparatuses, and administration.

This is Money's best DIY investing stages gather together, features a portion of our supported stages, and clarifies how their charging functions.

What amount Does It Cost to Buy and Sell Shares?

Expenses fluctuate as indicated by the administration you need. If you are simply buying or selling on the web–known as execution—just trading–level expenses can cost as meager as £2.50 or up to about £15. The more exchanges you do, the less expensive everyone is. Stamp obligation of 0.5 percent is charged on the acquisition of shares outside the lesser AIM market.

A few investors like to look for help from their brokers. Many offer 'optional' administrations, where they run an offering portfolio for your sake, just as 'advisory' administrations, where they offer exhortation. However, leave it to you to choose what to buy and sell and when. The more guidance you take, the more it costs.

Language Busting

- **The London Stock Exchange:** It is one of the fundamental markets. Huge, set up companies are recorded on this market, and they need to fulfill certain guidelines before they are permitted to go along with it.
- **Point:** Originally called the Alternative Investment Market. Likewise, part of the London Stock Exchange, it is intended for littler companies. The guidelines are less severe than for the Main Market, yet companies, despite everything, need to fulfill certain criteria before joining.
- **Income Stock:** Shares that deliver liberal dividends are known as income stocks since they furnish investors with a yearly income.
- **Growth Stock:**Fast-developing companies, regularly little and on AIM, are known as growth stocks. They once in a while, deliver a

profit.

- **Yield:** If you buy an offer at 100p and the organization delivers a profit of 5p, that offer is offering a 5% yield. The yield is determined by partitioning the profit by the offer cost and duplicating by 100.
- **Capital Gain:** If you buy an offer at 100p and sell it at 120p, the 20p that you have made is alluded to as a capital increase.

How Would I pick Which Stockbroker to Utilize?

This relies upon what administration you need. Investors who simply need to exchange online might be enticed to search out the least expensive supplier. That is fine, as long as the firm is managed by the Financial Conduct Authority.

A few investors may lean toward managing a firm whose name they perceive, and sites contrast as well, so it is critical to discover one that is anything but difficult to explore. Investors who are searching for counsel just as trading administrations should converse with a scope of brokers before settling on any firm choice. Search for a broker that you trust and regard.

To What Extent Would It Be a Good Idea for Me to Hold Shares?

Investors can be partitioned into traders and investors. Traders buy and sell shares as often as possible, planning to make speedy profits. Investors clutch their shares for, in any event, five years and, for the most part, significantly more.

Long haul investment in shares ought to demonstrate fulfilling, especially when investors reinvest their dividends to procure more shares. Some of the time, in any case, if an offer has risen fundamentally, investors may decide to sell a portion of their stock. This is known as top-cutting.

Will It Be Advisable for Me to Consider Before Buying?

The primary point to consider is whether you can bear to lose the money. Shares are not without risk investments, so on the off chance that you need the money to pay the home loan or school charges, track cautiously. It is additionally helpful to do your own examination.

Peruse an organization's most recent yearly report, take a gander at its site and look for counsel from your broker. Consider your investment points and your time skyline, as well. This will impact the sort of shares that you need to buy. Enormous, stable companies with conventional dividends will, in general, convey long haul rewards. Littler, riskier companies, can offer momentary energy.

If you do extravagant trading, as opposed to investing, it very well may be useful to set value targets with the goal that you sell probably a portion of your shares once you have made a profit.

When to Take Profits

Now and again, the choice to sell stocks is made for us, similar to the necessary least circulations retirees must take from their IRAs or 401(k)s consistently. That is a simple call to make—sponsored up by a weighty IRS punishment on the off chance that you don't. Yet, shouldn't something be said about the advantages left in that account, particularly stocks? When would it be a good idea for you to sell those?

All things considered, when an organization is declining in value with little no expectation of bounce back, it positively bodes well to sell. All things considered, we're saving capital. Be that as it may, the other circumstance—securing profits on a triumphant position—is progressively confused.

Profit-taking includes selling a triumphant situation to change over those restores into money. For instance, if I buy $1,000 worth of shares in XYZ Corporation, and the stock increases in value by half, I currently have a benefit worth $1,500. On the off chance that I sell $500 worth of that stock, I've changed over my benefits into a money profit. I despise everything that has $1,000 worth of XYZ shares, only less of them. Here are the situations when I would suggest doing that:

- When it's a great opportunity to rebalance your portfolio, at the point when at least one of your positions appreciates fast gains, you're rapidly going to withdraw from your objective designation, whatever it might be. Along these lines, you'll need to decrease your possessions in a triumphant stock.

- When the stock has arrived at a level and is probably going to "combine" inside a limited band for an all-encompassing period, I realize that sounds technical. However, it's quite basic. Most stocks will, in general, acknowledge in particular stages. In the combination stage, the value bobs between an upper opposition level and a lower bolster level. If the stock has a past filled with staying in the solidification stage for a long time, taking profits might be a smart thought.

Case of a union example and breakout:

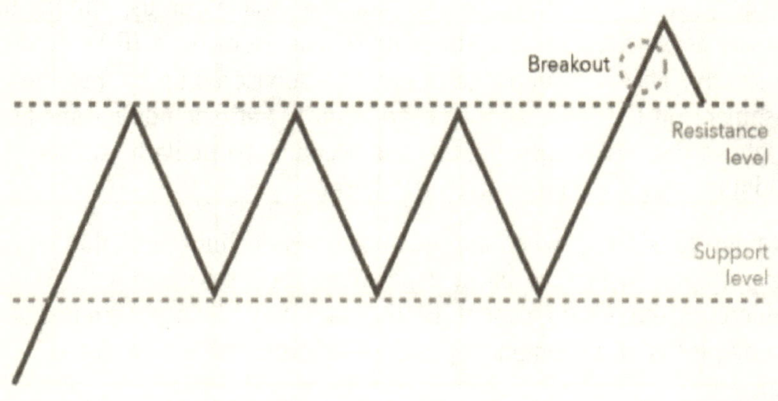

- To reuse profits into best-in-class stocks. Rather than having your money dallying through a union period, it very well may be winning new gains in another position. You could take your $500 gain on XYZ Corporation and use it to invest in a hot new growth organization that is going to appreciate a breakout.

Paradoxically, if a stock is encountering solid upward force, trading reliably over its 200-day moving normal, I'd keep it together to get the greatest additions conceivable. Hang tight for an affirmed move back toward the 200-day normal value level and take profits at that point. The perfect time to make out of here any stock—in the case of buying, selling, or taking profits—is the point at which the conditions are perfect.

Reliably distinguishing those conditions effectively takes research and experience—and a great deal of it. Distinguishing a feasible bullish breakout, an all-encompassing combination stage, or the perfect time to leave a position includes something other than perusing the features.

When to Sell Shares and Make the Most Profits to 20%

1. Take profits when your stock rises 20% to 25%
2. Expectations are taking off when you buy that incredible looking stock. In any case, in all actuality, not very many end up being beast achievers.
3. Except if the stock discloses to you else, you're best off taking probably a portion of your chips off the table when the stock ascents 20% or 25%.
4. Taking a few—or all—of your profit in that zone is a key sell rule. This is called an offensive deal: You're selling into quality, not into shortcoming.
5. The 20%-to-25% zone is anything but an irregular objective. The activity of numerous victors shows their conventions would peter be able to out at about that spot.
6. It doesn't mean the stock is dead (although it could be). Be that as it may, a type of genuine support and filling might be expected.
7. You can be additionally inspired by emptying at that gain if you see different issues begin to sneak in.

Perhaps the ongoing increases conveyed low volume. Possibly everyday trading ranges are getting excessively wide. Possibly the stock's business peers are beating. Might the stock prop up? Unquestionably. Be that as it may, at or close to 25%, your risk-reward proportion has moved fundamentally, and not in support of you. Presently you have this drawback to stress over. On the off chance that you aren't certain about the stock's upside, at that point, the proportion never again works for you.

Consider what happens when you sell that stock. You're raising money. If the market is in an uptrend, there ought to be another top-of-the-linestock inside the buying range. The stock you're selling ought to be a well past buying range. You're most likely trading your drained old pony for a crisp steed.

In any case, in some cases, your stock guides you to hang on. On the off chance that your stock ascents 20% inside three weeks of breaking out from a base or testing its 10-week moving normal, you should clutch that stock for an aggregate of about two months, at that point, choose to sell or hold for a more extended period. Large victors need time to create.

The most genuine test to this eight-week hold rule is the full circle rule: Don't let a twofold digit gain cycle into a misfortune. Is your eight-week-hold-rule stock transforming into a failure in the wake of rising over 10%? Sell.

Such a quickly rising stock is more a special case than the standard. Indeed, even among the market's best victors, you'll see a progression of 20%-to-25% advances, blended with retreats and base-building. Try not to think about this as a point of confinement to a stock's latent capacity, yet rather as an opportunity to allow it to pull together—and maybe continue its uptrend.

When to Sell Stock: Cut All Losses to a Limit of 7%

To bring in money in stocks, you should ensure the money you have. Live to invest one more day by adhering to this basic guideline: Always sell a stock if it falls 7%–8% beneath what you paid for it. No inquiries posed.

This essential standard encourages you to top your potential drawbacks. What's more, it's the least difficult approach to ensure you never let a little misfortune become a BIG one.

Why 7%–8%? The 7%–8% sell rule depends on our progressing study covering more than 130 years of stock market history.

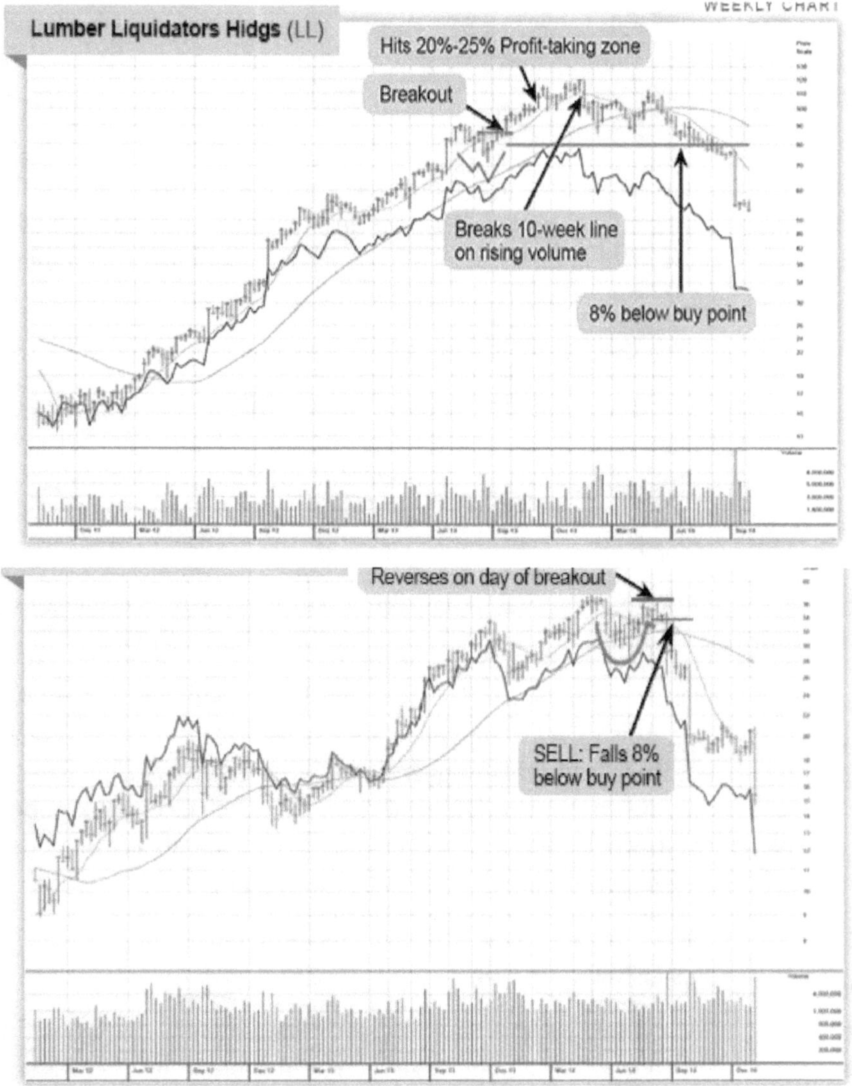

Indeed, even the best stocks will now and again break out and afterward drop to marginally beneath their optimal buy point. At the point when they do, they regularly don't fall over 8% beneath it. On the off chance that your stock declines over 8%, it, for the most part, implies something isn't right with your picked passage point, the organization, its industry, the general market, or the entirety of the above mentioned.

Here and there, you'll know the explanation. On different occasions, you won't. In any case, you do realize the stock is dropping, and you're perched on a 7%–8% misfortune. You should quickly move into a capital-safeguarding mode and cut that misfortune off.

When a stock starts to plunge hazardously, it's impossible to tell where the base is. Point of confinement your misfortune to 7% or 8% and get out. Envision a hatchet rushing through the air coming right at you. Okay, remain there attempting to make sense of things? Simply move to one side.

Your #1 need is to safeguard capital. Sell first, pose inquiries later.

Applying the 7%-8% Sell Rule If you buy a stock at 100 and it tumbles to 92 or 93, sell it. In any case, if that stock ascents to 150 and afterward slips 8% to $138, that doesn't trigger this specific sell rule, because the stock is as yet trading over your price tag. (Obviously, you might need to verify whether the stock is blazing some other admonition signs and sell signals.)

The 7%-8% Sell Rule in real-life Below are instances of why it's imperative to cut all losses rapidly.

Imagine a scenario in which you sell, and the stock rebounds and moves higher. There might be times when you sell a stock at a 7%–8% misfortune, just to see it bob back and move higher. While that can be baffling, make certain to keep things in context. Ordinarily, on the off chance that you buy accurately and your stock and the general market are acting great, your stock won't fall 7%–8% underneath the best possible buy point.

So, when the stock triggers that sell rule, make a move. Its conduct is revealing to you something isn't right.

Regardless of whether you sell at 8% misfortune and the stock rapidly bounce back, that doesn't mean you settled on an inappropriate choice. You were proactively securing your portfolio. Setting aside a little misfortune from the effort to time resembles paying a protection premium to ensure you don't endure an overwhelming hit. What's more, you can generally buy a stock back if it indeed shows quality.

HOW TO INVEST IN STOCKS, FOREX, AND SWING, DAY TRADING AND RELATED STRATEGIES

Forex Trading

The outside exchange market, likewise called the money market or forex (FX), is the world's biggest budgetary market, representing more than $4 trillion normal exchanged value every day. Contained banks, business companies, national banks, investment firms, mutual funds, and retail investors, the remote exchange market permits members to buy, sell, exchange, and estimate on monetary standards. There are various approaches to invest in the outside exchange market, including:

- **Forex.** The Forex market is a 24-hour money (spot) market where cash sets, for example, the Euro/US dollar (EUR/USD) pair, are exchanged. Since monetary standards are exchanged sets, investors and traders are basically wagering that one money will go up and the other will go down. The monetary standards are purchased and sold by the current cost or exchange rate.

- **Foreign cash fates.** These are prospects contracts on monetary forms, which are purchased and sold dependent on a standard size and repayment date. The CME Group is the biggest outside cash prospects market in the United States and offers fates contracts on G10 money matches just as developing market money sets and e-smaller scale items.

- **Foreign money options.** Where prospects contracts speak to a commitment to either buy or sell money sometimes not too far off, outside cash options give the option holder the right, however not the commitmentto buy or sell a fixed measure of remote money at a predefined cost at the very latest a predetermined date later on.

- **Exchange-exchanged funds (ETFs) and exchange-exchanged notes (ETNs).** Various outside cash exchange-exchanged items that give a presentation to remote exchange markets are accessible. A few ETFs are single-cash, while others buy and deal with a gathering of monetary standards.

- **Certificates of Deposit (CDs).** Outside cash CDs are accessible on singular monetary standards or bins of monetary standards and permit investors to acquire enthusiasm at remote rates. EverBank's"Reality Energy" container CD, for instance, offers a presentation to four monetary standards from non-Middle Eastern vitality delivering nations.

- **The Foreign Bond Funds**. These are the mutual funds that invest in the obligations of outside governments. Outside bonds are regularly named in the cash of the nation of the offer. On the off chance that the value of the outside cash rises comparative with the investor's neighborhood money, the earned premium will increment when it is changed over.

Swing Trading

Swing traders are essentially traders that exchange the multi-day to multi-week time allotment. They, for the most part, take a shot at four-hour (H4) and day by day (D1) charts, and they may utilize a mix of fundamental examination and technical investigation to manage to trade their choices.

Regardless of whether there is a long-haul trend or whether the market is, to a great extent, territory bound, it doesn't generally make a difference. A Forex swing merchant won't clutch a position long enough for it totally altogether.

Rather, instability is the key for swing traders. The more unstable the market is, the more noteworthy the quantity of transient value developments, and this makes more open doors for swing trading.

What Are the Benefits of Swing Trading?

There are various advantages to swing trading, particularly for new traders.

Swing Trading Requires Less Time

As noted, very transient exchanges require steady observing. Then again, long haul exchanges may not be dynamic enough for a great many people and require a ton of trading discipline.

Swing trading will, in general, intrigue to the mentality of a learner, just because it utilizes aneasier to understand time allotment. Swing traders invest considerably less energy investigating and trading as they are doing fewer exchanges than hawkers over a longer period. This gives them more opportunity to consider and put their positions, yet additionally implies they just need to put a day shortly making exchanges.

Swing Trading Exploits Longer Trends

While scalping and day trading depends on transient instability, swing trading permits traders to exploit week by week, month to month, and yearly trends.

This thusly implies swing trading may offer preferred outcomes over day trading because the examination will be increasingly important. Investigations performed on bigger units of time are regularly more grounded examinations, though shorter-term trading is progressively powerless against bogus signs. It likewise implies that each exchange has more opportunity to create a profit because of exchanges following longer swings costs.

Swing Trading Is More Cost Proficient

One of the primary expenses of trading is the spread, or the distinction between the buy and sell cost of an advantage. While spreads are an exceptionally limited quantity, they do get charged each time you make an exchange, which implies it can altogether eat into the profits of ultra-momentary trading.

For swing traders, the spread doesn't generally make a difference because the exchanges occur after some time scales so wide that a spread of a couple of focuses or pips doesn't fundamentally cut into profits.

Swing Traders Can Utilize a Scope of Indicators

The swing trading time units-four-hourly, every day, and week after week makes it conceivable to take advantage of the least difficult indicators. Surely, if we take the case of a day-by-day candle shutting over the 20-time frame moving normal, it's substantially more agent than a similar candle shutting over the moving normal on a 5-minute chart. At last, higher time allotments are progressively precise, and swing traders can profit from this.

Utilizing MetaTrader 4 and 5 Supreme Edition, it's anything but difficult to investigate different time units on a solitary diagram or various, where the Mini Chart pointer permits you to show at least two-time units of a solitary instrument simultaneously. To become familiar with MetaTrader Supreme Edition, and download it for FREE, click the pennant beneath!

Swing Traders Can Abuse Bigger Value Developments

Swing traders can abuse huge value developments or motions that would be hard to acquire during a day. The more unpredictable the market, the more noteworthy the swings will be, and the more noteworthy the quantity of swing trading openings.

Risks Related to Swing Trading

While swing trading has a scope of advantages, it likewise accompanies a few risks. They are:

• The amassing of swap expenses: Swaps are a day-by-day loan fee that is charged on places that are held medium-term. While these aren't an issue for hawkers or day traders, these charges can include longer-term exchanges.

• Fundamental risk: Economic and political occasions during the end of the week could influence the money related markets at the opening, which can lose a trend and upset your trading methodology.

The Best Instruments for Swing Trading

So which markets would you be able to swing exchange? Fortunately, this trading style is conceivable on all CFD instruments, including stocks, Forex, items, and even lists.

In the Forex market, swing trading permits traders to profit by brilliant liquidity, enough instability to get intriguing value moves, all inside a generally brief timeframe outline. Probably the most famous monetary forms for Forex swing trading are:

- Euro: Pairs incorporate the AUD/EUR, EUR/CAD, EUR/JPY, and EUR/GBP
- Japanese Yen: Pairs incorporate the USD/JPY, JPY/CAD, and JPY/GBP.
- British Pound: Pairs incorporate the GBP/AUD, GBP/CAD, and GBP/CHF.
- US Dollar: Pairs incorporate the NZD/USD, USD/CAD, AUD/USD, and EUR/USD.

For stock market swing trading, records are additionally exceptionally alluring instruments. These include:

- The DAX30 CFD
- The CAC40 CFD
- The Dow Jones 30 CFD
- The Nasdaq 100 CFD
- The Nikkei 225 CFD

Some stock records have bigger spreads than different instruments, for example, Forex sets, they are frequently a decent resource for swing trading, just because you just need to pay for the spread once. The equivalent goes for fascinating money sets, for example, the USDCZK.

The Most Effective Method to Begin Swing Trading

Are you anxious, to begin with, swing trading? Fortunately, you can begin with the accompanying advances:

1. Open a swing trading account: You can see the full procedure for opening a record in our article How to open a MetaTrader 5 record.
2. Download and introduce your trading stage: Either MetaTrader 4

or MetaTrader 5.

3. **Open the stage and make your first exchange:** Now, you have to pick a benefit and open your first exchange

Day Trading

Forex Day Trading Systems, Strategies and Tips

This book will give traders meanings of day trading and intraday trading. It will investigate diverse day trading systems, how traders make profits with day trading systems, a few recommendations for the best Forex day trading systems, and some valuable tips for you to use in your everyday trading.

Intra-day trading is a lot of Forex day trading strategies that request proficient traders to open and close exchanges around the same time. Taking into account that markets can just move so far inside one day, intra-day traders utilize moderately riskier trading strategies to amass their ideal profits.

Day trading Forex strategies are more activity stuffed and expect traders to be available at the trading station all through the session. It's broadly acknowledged that the smaller a time a dealer works inside, the more risk they are probably going to be presented to. That is the reason day trading can be depicted as probably the riskiest way to deal with the money markets.

It's not so much the distinctive Forex trading strategies that day traders need to utilize that expands the risk. The general-rationale is the equivalent for practically any interim out there. It is that Forex day trading rules will, in general, be increasingly cruel and unforgiving to the individuals who don't tail them.

Strategies

The two factors that no intra-day representative can oversee without – irrelevant of the Forex day exchanging rule they hope to use–are unconventionality and liquidity. However, transient traders are unquestionably increasingly subject to them. Instability is the size of market developments. When trading at the present moment, strong instability is an absolute necessity.

This essentially decreases the choice of instruments to the significant cash sets and a couple of cross sets, contingent upon the sessions. Discussing sessions, since instability is session dependent, realizing when to exchange is as significant as comprehending what to exchange. Liquidity is similarly significant. Intra-day trading is exceptionally exact. A long-haul broker can stand to toss in 10 pips here and cut 10 pips there. A transient dealer can't because 10 pips could be the entire profit anticipated for an exchange.

This accuracy in Forex originates from the dealer's aptitude obviously; however, rich liquidity is significant as well. If there is no liquidity, the requests will just not close at the ideal value, regardless of how great the merchant is—this by and by limits intraday traders to a specific arrangement of trading instruments and trading times.

Scalping

Scalping is a day exchanging Forex strategy that intends to achieve various little benefits reliant on the irrelevant worth changes that may occur. Sellers go for sum trades, opening about 'on a hunch,' considering the way that there is no other strategy to investigate through the market upheaval. Scalping can be stimulating and, all the while, unsafe. Peddlers must achieve high exchanging probability to change the for the most part safe to compensate extent. In all probability, the hardest bit of scalping is closing losing trades time.

A peddler essentially can't stand to believe that the market will return.

In case you are hoping to transform into a vendor, consider developing a sixth market sense—scan for flighty instruments, incredible liquidity, and impeccable execution speed. At whatever point aced, scalping is possibly the most gainful method in any budgetary market. It is only the abutting dangers that shield it from being the best Forex day exchanging methodology.

Modify Trading

An instance of modifying exchanging using the Stochastic marker. Disclaimer: Charts for financial instruments right now for illustrative purposes and doesn't contain exchanging urging or a mentioning to purchase or sell any cash related instrument gave by Admiral Markets (CFDs, ETFs, Shares). Past execution isn't generally an indication of future execution. Switch exchanging is, in any case, called pullback exchanging, counter-pattern exchanging, and obscuring.

The hazard begins with the key standard of exchanging against the pattern. A switch shipper must have the alternative to recognize potential pullbacks with a high probability, similarly to have the choice to anticipate their quality. Regardless of the way that surely possible, it requires a lot of market data and practice. The 'Step by step Pivots' approach can be seen as a one-of-a-kind occasion of the switch exchanging framework, as it invests noteworthy energy in exchanging each day low and step by step high pullbacks and pivots.

Power Trading

This is an extremely clear day exchanging Forex method that works in filtering for strong worth moves coordinated with high volumes and exchanging toward the move. A raised degree of exchanging discipline is required in power exchanging, to have the choice to believe that the best open entryway will enter a position, and keep up solid control to keep focus and perceive the left sign.

Day exchanging is every now and again exposed as the snappiest technique to make an appearance on your interest in Forex exchanging. In any case, what the adverts disregard to refer to is that it's the most problematic framework to pro. As needs are, various beginner dealers endeavor to miss the mark. Through significant stretches of learning and getting understanding, a specialist vendor may develop an individual framework for Forex day exchanging.

The Forex Day Trading Systems

Forex day trading is carefully done inside one day, and exchanges are constantly shut before the market closes on that equivalent day. The individuals who exchange thusly are alluded to as day traders. A Forex day trading framework is normally involved a lot of technical signs, which influence the choices made by the broker concerning buying or selling on every one of their day-by-day sessions. The framework can assist traders with navigating the market considerably more productively and unquestionably, with the point of permitting them to acquire profit.

Previously, the movement of Forex day trading was restricted to monetary associations and expert examiners. Most of the day, traders were the representatives of banks or investment firms, who worked in value investment and funded the board. In any case, with the presentation of electronic trading and edge trading systems, the day trading framework has now picked up ubiquity among 'at-home traders.'

With simple access to Forex trading, presently, nearly anybody can exchange Forex from the solace of their own homes. Individuals decide to go into day trading for different reasons. Be that as it may, a factor which is probably going to have made this action significantly more well-known over the late years is the way that day traders don't acquire the 'swap,' which is a charge that is brought about when a position is kept open medium-term.

How Do Forex Day Traders Make Profit?

Day traders influence huge aggregates of cash-flow to make profits by profiting by little value changes among the exceptionally fluid indexes, stocks, or monetary standards. In that capacity, these brokers are not looking for gigantic dunks and tops in the expenses. Or maybe, they are content with pretty much nothing, moderate advancements. In any case, their trade sizes are more prominent than the ones asserted by dealers that contribute over longer periods. As a day expedite, the rule point is to make an impressive proportion of pips inside a particular day.

Ideally, you should make returns on both the highs and lows of the focal points. The sections in the diverse Forex day trading systems utilize comparative sorts of instruments that are used in typical trading-the main distinction is in the planning and approach. With day trading, you by and large hope to make less profit per exchange, yet you hope to accomplish unquestionably more exchanges.

THE STOCK MARKET INVESTING CHART

I f you're going to effectively exchange stocks as a stock market investor, at that point, you have to realize how to peruse stock charts. Indeed, even traders who essentially utilize fundamental investigation to choose stocks to invest in still frequently utilize technical examination of stock value development to decide explicit buy or section, and sell, or leave, focuses.

Stock charts are unreservedly accessible on sites, for example, Google Finance and Yahoo Finance, and stock brokerages consistently make stock charts accessible for their customers. So, you shouldn't experience any difficulty discovering stock charts to analyze.

Stock Chart Construction – Lines, Bars, Candlesticks

Stock charts can change in their development from bar charts to candle charts to line charts to point and figure charts. Almost all stock charts give you the option to switch between the different sorts of charts, just as the capacity to overlay different technical indicators on a chart. You can likewise differ the time span appeared by a chart. While day by day charts are presumably the most ordinarily utilized, intraday, week by week, month to month, year-to-date (YTD), 5-year, 10-year, and a total authentic lifetime of stock are likewise accessible.

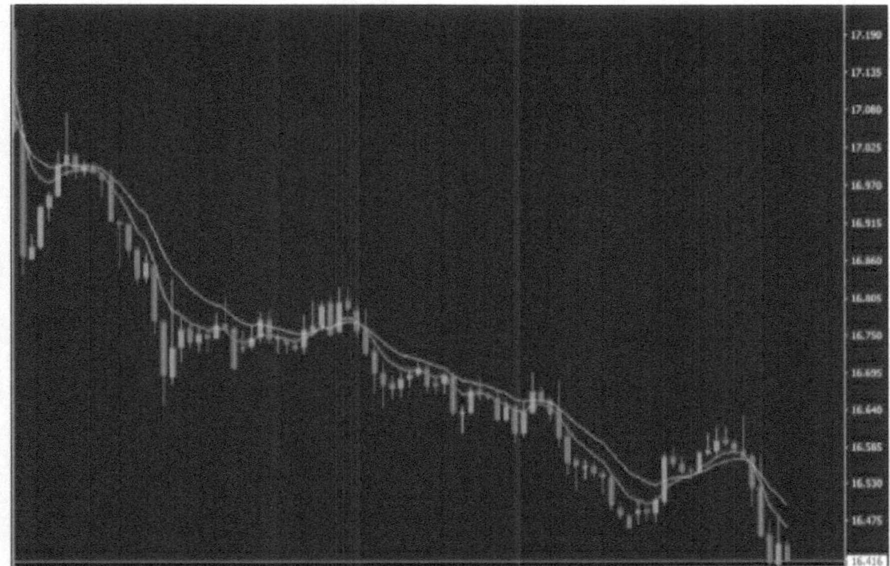

There are relatively favorable circumstances and inconveniences to utilizing diverse chart development styles and to utilizing distinctive time allotments for examination. What style and time span will work best for you as an individual examiner or investor is something that you can just find through really doing a stock chart examination. You can gather important signs of plausible stock value development from any stock chart. You ought to pick the chart style that makes it almost effortless for you to peruse and break down the chart and exchange profitably.

Taking a Gander at a Stock Chart

The following is a year-to-date day-by-day chart of Apple Inc. (AAPL), civility of stockcharts.com. This chart is a candle chart, with white candles showing up days for the stock and red candles appearing down days. What's more, this chart has a few technical indicators included: a 50-period moving normal and a 200-period moving normal, showing up as blue and red lines on the chart; the relative quality pointer (RSI) which shows up in a different window over the primary chart window; the moving normal intermingling difference marker (MACD) which shows up in a different window underneath the chart.

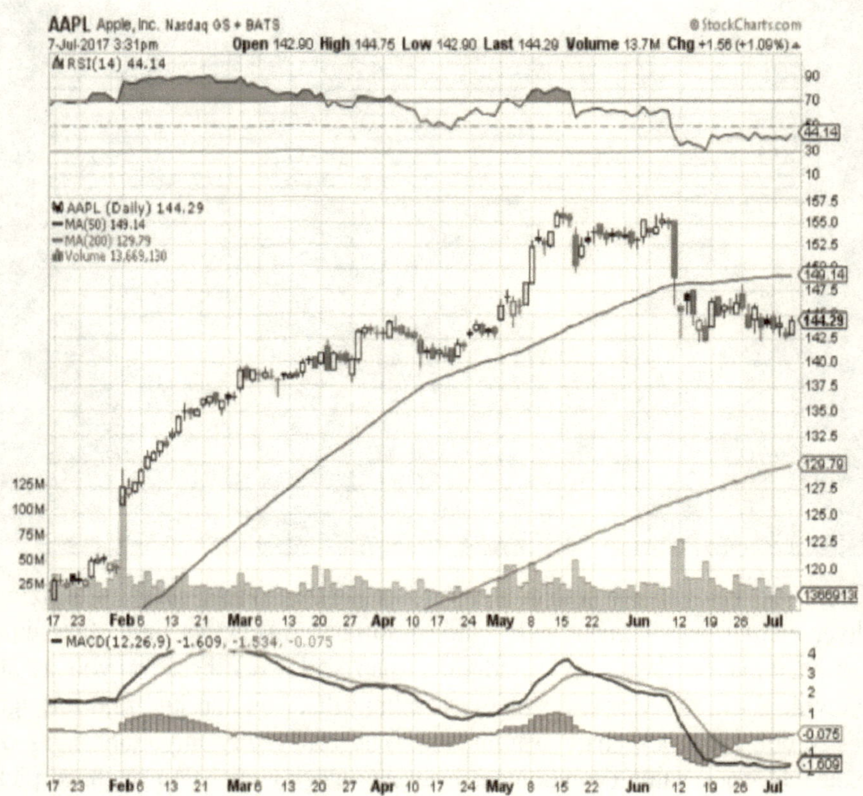

Along the base of the principal chart window, the day-by-day trading volume appears. Note the huge spike in volume that happened on February first, when the stock gapped higher and started a solid uptrend, which went on until early June.

Likewise, note the high measure of selling volume (shown by red volume bars, which demonstrate days with a more noteworthy measure of selling volume than buying volume). That happens when the stock moves strongly downward around June twelfth.

The Importance of Volume

The volume shows up on almost every stock chart that you'll discover. That is because trading volume is viewed as a basic technical marker by about each stock investor. On the chart above, notwithstanding demonstrating all out-degree of trading volume for every day, days with more noteworthy buying volume are shown with blue bars, and days with more noteworthy selling volume are shown with red bars.

The explanation that volume is viewed as a significant technical pointer is a basic one. Most by far of stock market buying and selling is finished by enormous institutional traders, for example, investment banks, and by fund supervisors, for example, mutual fund or exchange-exchanged fund (ETF) chiefs. At the point when those investors make significant buys or offers of stock, it makes high trading volume, and it is that sort of significant buying and selling by enormous investors that ordinarily move a stock sequential.

Consequently, individual or other institutional traders watch volume figures for signs of significant buying or selling action by enormous foundations. This data can be utilized either to gauge a future value trend for the stock or to distinguish key-value backing and opposition levels.

Indeed, numerous individual investors decide their buying and selling choices exclusively dependent on following the recognized activities of major institutional traders. They buy stocks when volume and value development show that significant establishments are buying and sell or abstain from buying stocks when there is major institutional selling.

Such a system works best when applied to significant stocks that are commonly intensely exchanged. It will probably be less powerful when applied to stocks of little companies that are not yet on the radar screens of enormous institutional investors and that have moderately little trading volumes even on days when the stock is more vigorously exchanged than expected.

Essential Volume Patterns

There are four essential volume designs that traders regularly watch as indicators.

High volume trading on Up Days – This is a bullish sign that a stock's cost will keep on rising.

Low volume trading on Down Days – This is additionally a bullish sign since it shows that on days when the stock's value falls back a piece, relatively few investors are engaged with the trading. In this way, such down days happening in a general bull market are normally deciphered as impermanent retracements or amendments instead of as indicators of future huge value development.

High Volume Trading on Down Days – This is viewed as a bearish pointer for a stock, as it shows that major institutional traders are forcefully selling the stock.

Low Volume Trading on Up Days – This is another bearish pointer, although not as solid as high-volume trading on down days. The low volume will, in general, peg the trading activity on such days as less huge and, for the most part, proof of only a momentary counter-trend retracement upward in an in general, long haul bearish trend.

Utilizing Technical Indicators

In dissecting stock charts for stock market investing, investors utilize an assortment of technical indicators to help them all the more exactly likely value development, to recognize trends, and to envision market inversions from bullish trends to bearish trends and the other way around.

One of the most normally utilized technical indicators is moving normally. The moving midpoints that are most much of the time applied to day-by-day stock charts are the 20-day, 50-day, and 200-day moving normally. By and large, talking up to a shorter period moving normal is over a more drawn-out period moving normal, a stock is viewed as in a general uptrend. On the other hand, if shorter-term moving midpoints are beneath longer-term moving midpoints, at that point, that demonstrates a general downtrend.

The Importance of the 200-Day Moving Average

The 200-day moving normal is considered by most experts as a basic marker on a stock chart. Traders who are bullish on a stock need to see the stock's cost stay over the 200-day moving normally. Bearish traders who are selling short a stock need to see the stock value remain underneath the 200-day moving normally. If a stock's value crosses from underneath the 200-day moving normal to above it, this is generally deciphered as a bullish market inversion. A drawback cross of cost from over the 200-day moving normal is deciphered as a bearish sign for the stock.

Also, the interchange between the 50-and-200-day moving midpoints is considered as a solid marker for future value development. At the point when the 50-day normal moving crosses from beneath to over the 200-day normal moving, the technical investigators allude to this as a "brilliant cross." A brilliant cross is essentially a sign that the stock is "gold," set at significantly greater expenses.

On the other side, if the 50-day moving normal crosses from above to beneath the 200-day moving normal, this is alluded to by experts as a "demise cross." You can presumably make sense of on your own that a "passing cross" isn't considered to look good at a stock's future cost development.

Trend and Momentum Indicators

There are intents and purposes an interminable rundown of technical indicators for traders to look over in breaking down a chart. Examination with different indicators to find the ones that work best for your specific style of trading, and as applied to the particular stocks that you exchange. You'll likely locate that a few indicators work very well for you in gauging value development for certain stocks yet for nobody else.

Technical examiners frequently use indicators of various kinds related to one another. Technical indicators are characterized into two fundamental sorts: trend indicators, for example, moving midpoints, and energy indicators, for example, the MACD or the normal directional list (ADX). Trend indicators are utilized to distinguish the general course of a stock's cost, up or down, while energy indicators check the quality of value development.

Dissecting Trends

While checking on a stock chart, notwithstanding deciding the stock's general trend, up or down, it's additionally useful to hope to distinguish parts of a trend, for example, the accompanying:

- How long has a trend been set up? Stocks don't remain in uptrends or downtrends uncertainly. In the end, there are consistently trend changes. On the off chance that a trend has proceeded for an extensive time with no huge remedial retracement moves the other way, you need to be particularly alert for indications of an approaching market inversion.

- How does a stock will in general exchange? A few stocks move in generally moderate, very much characterized trends. Different stocks will, in general, experience greater unpredictability all the time, with value making sharp go up or down even amidst a general long-haul trend. Ifyou are trading a stock that normally confirms high unpredictability, at that point, you know not to put an excess of significance on the trading activity in any single day.

- Are there indications of a potential trend inversion? Cautious investigation of stock value development regularly uncovers indications of potential trend inversions. Energy indicators regularly show a trend coming up short on steam before the cost of stock really tops, allowing ready traders the chance to escape a stock at a decent cost before it switches to the drawback. A different candle or other chart designs are likewise frequently used to distinguish significant market inversions.

Distinguishing Support and Resistance Levels

Stock charts can be especially useful in distinguishing backing and obstruction levels for stocks. Bolster levels are value levels where you are normally observing crisp buying coming in to help a stock's cost and turn it back to the upside. Then again, obstruction levels speak to costs at which a stock has demonstrated a propensity to flop in endeavoring to move higher, turning around to the drawback.

Recognizing backing and opposition levels can be particularly useful in trading a stock that will, in general, exchange inside a setup trading range over an extensive stretch of time. Some stock traders, having distinguished such a stock, will hope to buy the stock at help levels and sell it at obstruction levels, again and again, getting increasingly more cash as the stock navigates a similar ground on numerous occasions.

For stocks that have very much recognized help and opposition levels, value breakouts past both of those levels can be significant indicators of future value development. For instance, if a stock has recently neglected to break above $50 an offer, however, then at long last do as such, this might be an indication that the stock will move from that point to a significantly more significant expense level.

The chart of General Electric (GE) underneath shows that the stock exchanged a tight range somewhere in the range of $29 and $30 an offer for a while. However, once the stock cost broke beneath the $29 bolster level, it kept on falling considerably lower.

End–Using Stock Chart Analysis

Stock chart investigation isn't dependable, not even in the hands of the most master technical expert. On the off chance that it was, each stock investor would be a multi-mogul. Be that as it may, figuring out how to peruse a stock chart will help turn the chances of being a fruitful stock market investor in support of you.

Stock chart examination is an ability, and like some other expertise, one just turns into a specialist at it through training. Fortunately, practically anybody ready to work perseveringly at dissecting stock charts can become, if not a through and through the master, in any event truly great at it–adequate to improve their general profitability in stock market trading. Along these lines, it's to your greatest advantage as an investor to start, or proceed, your instruction in stock chart examination.

HOW MUCH TO INVEST IN THE STOCK MARKET?

How to Begin with Stocks

Investing, even in limited quantities, can receive huge benefits. Here are six different ways you can begin investing with minimal expenditure today. For some individuals, "investing" evokes pictures of men in suits, observing the exchange of a great many dollars on a stock ticker.

I'm here to let you know you don't should be the Wolf of Wall Street to begin investing. It's alright in case you're, to a greater extent, a mouse of Main Street. Regardless of whether you just have a couple of dollars to save, your money will develop with accumulated dividends.

The way to building riches is growing acceptable propensities—like consistently taking care of money consistently. Swap out the barista-made cappuccinos for espresso at home, and you could, as of now, be spared more than $50 every month.

1. Attempt the Treat Container Approach

Putting aside money and contributing it is immovably related. In order to put away cash, you at first need to save some up. That will take altogether less time than you may presume, and you can do it in little advances.

If you've never been a saver, you can start by dealing with just $10 consistently. That may not seem, by all accounts, to be a lot; in any case, through the range of a year, it comes to over $500.

Try putting $10 into an envelope, shoebox, somewhat secured, or even that mind-boggling bank of the primary lodging, the treat holder. Despite the way, this may sound silly; it's consistently a significant beginning advance. Get yourself into the inclination for living on to some degree shy of what you get, and stash the save finances away in an ensured spot.

Discover Bank, as of now, offers a strong 1.60% APY on its online venture account. There is no store required and no month-to-month bolster costs (or various charges) identified with a Discover Bank online speculation account, so the yield is earned on all modifies.

The brand, in like manner, offers exceptional yield CDs, checking, and currency advertise accounts, so if you have to expand your store's portfolio a dab, Discover Bank has a lot of what you need. What may be contrasted with the treat compartment is the online ledger; it's not quite the same as your monetary records. The cash can be pulled in two business days in case you need it, yet it's not associated with your plastic. By then, when the save is adequately colossal, you can take it out and move it into some certifiable venture vehicles.

Start with unassuming amounts of cash, and a short time later augmentation as you get progressively OK with the rule. It may include deciding not to go to McDonald's or passing on the movies, and putting that cash into the treat holder.

Save that money to be invested immediately? Oak seeds are an application that gathers together your credit and platinum card buys and invests the distinction. It's not extravagant, yet it's a beginning. Also, for individuals who've never been savers, understanding that start is even more significant.

2. Let a Robo-Advisor Invest Your Money for You

Robo-advisors were made to make investing as basic and open as could be allowed. No earlier investment experience is required, and the set-up is simple. Let their computerized insight track your investments out of sight and pay lower expenses all the while.

Partner Invest

Partner Invest is a Robo-advisor I energetically prescribe to first-time investors on the off chance that you'd like some help dealing with your money and investments. There are no advisory expenses, yearly charges, or rebalancing expenses.

After you determine your investment objectives, Ally's group of human masters alters your portfolio for the correct equalization of risk and return that you're generally OK with. Furthermore, you can follow your exhibition day in and day out with Ally's online instruments, which are anything but difficult to utilize.

Wealthfront

Another mind-boggling, Robo-consultant that I recommend to first-time speculators is Wealthfront. Their costs are reasonable at 0.25%. In any case, the kicker is that you can get your first $5,000 regulated free (express to MU30 perusers).

So, on the off chance that you're planning to start contributing with negligible consumption, Wealthfront could be the best methodology. You will require $500 to start notwithstanding, considering Wealthfront, so keep that.

M1 Finance

If you don't have that $500 starting balance, there are, up until now, exceptional alternatives for you in the Robo-admonishing space. You can investigate one of their pre-made expanded portfolios or change your own by purchasing stocks and ETFs through their establishment. The UI is too easy even to consider utilizing.

3. Make Your Initial Phases Inland Market

Land investing doesn't need to be for the extremely rich. There are numerous options for land crowdfunding, and however, this may appear as though something you'd be apprehensive about investigating – it really can be a fascinating investment.

With Fundrise's extremely simple to-utilize online stage, you just need a beginning least investment of $500. So, in case you're an unaccredited investor, you can buy properties without paying those exceptionally huge charges that wind up being a major issue if you need to begin fiddling with the land. The expenses come to simply 1% by dealing with your own portfolio and Fundraise consistently offers a 90 days' fulfillment ensure.

4. Take a Crack at Your Boss' Retirement Plan

In case you're on a strict budget, even the basic advance of taking a crack at your 401(k) or other boss retirement plan may appear past your range. Yet, there is a way that you can start investing in a business supported retirement plan with sums that are so little you won't notice them.

For example, plan to contribute just 1% of your compensation to the marketable strategy. You likely won't miss a dedication that little, yet what makes it a lot less difficult is that the cost finds that you'll get for doing so will make the responsibility significantly tinier.

At the point when you center on a 1% responsibility, you can extend it logically consistently. For example, in year two, you can grow your pledge to 2% of your pay. In year three, you can assemble your promise to 3%of your pay, and so on.

In case you time the additions with your yearly pay increment, you'll notice the extended duty even less. So, in case you get a 2% compensation raise, it will suitably be separating the development between your retirement plan and your money related records. Also, if your administrator gives an organizing board of trustees, that will make the game arrangement incredibly better.

Blooom is an unprecedented gadget for hands-off speculation, the leading body of your 401(k). Immediately, they'll give you a free 401(k) examination, unveiling to you where and how they can propel your ventures.

5. Put Your Cash in Low-Starting Speculation Common Assets

Shared assets are speculation assurances that license you to put resources into a game plan of stocks and protections with a single trade, making them perfect for new financial specialists.

The trouble is various common reserve organizations require beginning least speculations of someplace in the scope of $500 and $5,000. On the off chance that you're a first-time financial specialist with insignificant use to contribute, those fundamentals can be far off. Regardless, some shared store organizations will defer the record fundamentals if you agree to a modified month to month ventures of someplace in the scope of $50 and $100.

Modified contributing is a commonplace component with shared reserve and ETF IRA accounts. It's less customary with assessable records. In any case, it's continually worth inquisitive concerning whether it's available. Shared reserve organizations that have been known to do this consolidate Dreyfus, Transamerica, and T. Rowe Price.

A modified contributing strategy is particularly invaluable if you can do it through money save reserves. You can usually set up a modified store condition through your account, comparatively that you do with a business bolstered retirement plan. Basically, ask your HR division how to set it up.

6. Keep away from All Dangers with Treasury Securities

Generally, not many little financial specialists start their speculation adventure with US Treasury assurances. Be that as it may, you can. You'll never get rich with these assurances, yet it is an extraordinary spot to stop your cash—and increase some eagerness—until you are good to go into higher hazard/better yield ventures and Bonds

For as small as $10, you can put resources into Worthy Bonds. Estimable Bonds are fixed interest protections that store propels for dependable American associations. The protections have a term of three years, yet the premium is paid step by step, and you can pull back your cash at whatever point, without discipline. Purchase a similar number of $10 bonds as you'd like.

The essential idea is that Worthy is going to take the cash you use to purchase protections and put it into organizations with a more imperative return than 5%. They win, you win, and it's a fixed rate, so you know the pace of return every day.

The stage is accessible to all U.S. financial specialists and can be a mind-blowing technique to grow your portfolio with, for the most part,a safe plan. Honorable simply put resources into totally ensured about advances (liquid assets having worth in a general sense more noticeable than the development entirety), so the idea of credit and venture is for each situation high measure.

Rundown

There isplenty of ways to deal with start contributing with negligible use, with various on the web and application-based stages, making it less difficult than whenever in ongoing memory. You ought to just start somewhere. At the point when you do, it will get less difficult as time goes on, and your future self will love you for it.

Insider Facts of the Stock Market

Your best and just wager is to confide in your own insight and self consistently, particularly with regards to your money. Along these lines, you should know the insider facts altogether behind the market on the off chance that you are to win reliably or succeed by any means. The people pulling strings don't need you to know reality with regards to the stock market in any event, for an expense regardless of how high.

Additionally, the stockbrokers are obliged to their Brokerages and get significantly more cash-flow with fat commissions from the enormous exchanges of the huge folks. So, it isn't to their greatest advantage to direct you accurately. Or maybe they will control their recommendation to you the incorrect way, because your misfortune is the success of the enormous folks. It's all personal circumstances. So be careful with the Stockbrokers' recommendation. It leaves you with no decision; however, to know reality with regards to the Stock Market.

1. The first target ought to be the protection of the head. Next comes profits. You can bring in money the two different ways-going up or down, insofar as you wager the correct way. Things you hear in the open about the market are frequently plum off-base. Truth be told, they are actually something contrary to what's valid.

It's straightforward. We tell you the best way to piggy-back yourself with the Big Guys. Do what they do. The key is to discover what the huge folks are doing and do precisely that. Ride here and there with them. The best approach to discover what the enormous folks do is by taking a gander at the ticker tape and watch for huge square movement. At that point, read the charts of the stock or product. That is the workmanship in itself. The charts uncover a great deal.

The charts to be contemplated are 1 day, 2 days, 3 days, 5 days, week, month, and if need be, a year or more. The web has all the data you need about any item or stock on the off chance that you have the tolerance. The more you study, the better choice you can make about awareness or stock. It's everything in the charts. Chart arrangements additionally are significant. Each Chart Formation has its own story to tell. In any case, duplicity hides at each corner.

There are no ensures. Try not to let it alarm you. We will make you see through the misdirection. At that point, likewise, take a gander at day by day, week by week, month to month and yearly all out buying and selling action otherwise called Volume.

2. The stock market is likewise about psychology and mind control. The market producers utilize each means available to them at making overpowering feelings and psy-operations that they use with the most extreme mechanical exactness. They will utilize explanations from soothsaying to black magic to superstitions to old housewives' stories, even fantasies to accomplish their objective of deluding you. The market creators are the proverbial 'house' as in Casinos. The stock market is savage on the consistent lurk to part you with your money. The stock market is the number one world's greatest Casino. Just the individuals who can see through this double-dealing will win.

At that point, there is a procedure. The more cautious you are, the less risk you take, and the less money you gain the ground yet is forward. The more you take a risk, the more the odds of losing and losing huge. You don't need that. You need to win consistently and without a doubt.

At the point when you join the Abovementioned-Research, Charts, Psychology, and Skill/Strategy, winning is improved and guaranteed. This is only our aim for you. The ideas we show are material for the two stocks commodities, whether you are day-trading or investing in putting it plainly, medium, or long haul.

3. The individuals accountable for making and moving the market are called Specialists. They sit close and work with the 'floor brokers' of the exchanges. The Specialists are responsible for around 40 or

so stocks in the NY Stock Exchange. The Specialist work for the significant investors of the companies recorded in the stock exchanges. The Specialists do as they are told by these equivalent Shareholders. They do things any other way pretty much inevitably; however, their hidden reason and goal is consistently the equivalent-to lose you and take your money.

4. You ought to likewise acclimate yourself with the propensities for the market creators-things they do and for what reason and anticipate what they will do straightaway. That is something you can't contemplate in a day, month, or even a year. We will disclose to all of you about that. Our total experience traverses over 60 years right now.

The undulations of the market are not erratic. They have implications. For instance, when the market goes up toward the beginning of the day, it implies a certain something, and when it goes up close to the center of the day, it implies something different, and when it goes up tothe early evening, it once more, implies something so different. Each undulation has reason and importance.

Regardless of whether you are a day-broker or quite a while investor, there is an opportunity to pause and sit idle. That is an opportunity to watch and see what 'they' are up to and set up. You likewise need to realize when to hop in (to open an exchange) the market at the specific picked time. At that point, there is the absolute time to jump out (close the exchange). It's just as simple as that. There lies the test.

5. Contrary to what individuals accept, the Stock Exchange doesn't take part in an auction market where the most noteworthy bidder gets the stock. Or maybe, its activities are actually the inverse. Individuals hop in the market when Specialists raise the cost of stock and the other way around. You understand the greatness of this disclosure; just when you find a workable pace, the Stock Market is the place the Specialists are the 'Wizard of Oz' calling the shots behind blinds of a phase.

6. The stock market is the same as common retail and discount merchanting activity. Similarly, as in buying in discount and selling in retail, such is crafted by the Specialists. On the off

chance that you can stay this in your brain and use it as a rudder, you can explore the stock market situation securely and profitably. As the stock costs are raised by Specialists, they tidy up their books in their equal stock records and dispose of their stock. It's everything about profits. The stocks are first offered to the 'most loved pet children and afterward to the conciliatory whipping boys(goats). Precisely the same methodology is rehashed backward when the stocks are going down in the last case selling as opposed to buying. It will be ideal if you pardon my mockery. It is simply to indicate my expected implications.

You must be brilliant to have the option to figure out the real story. You must be astute if you need to dominate in his match. Keenness and the right planning are all you need. On the off chance that you can time your passageways and exits in your open a shut position, you have it split. When you decode this code, it will all be the presence of mind to you. You would then be able to get out from under your enthusiastic propensities, which are consistently in a struggle with what is truly going on.

www.ingramcontent.com/pod-product-compliance
Lightning Source LLC
Chambersburg PA
CBHW022007170726
47994CB00023B/2418